AN IRISH REBEL IN NEW SPAIN

Pregon de los Justos
Justicia de Dios.
que castigue a quien lo quitare.

L_10_   8

Yo Don Guillen Lombardo reuocando como reuoco el emplaçamiento que hize de mis agrauios an...
a Dios, protesto en su prission ... en la de los angeles y hombres, que no son grata a los ... mis ...
son integros porque Dios nro señor los castiga en la otra vida, sino para su emienda sobre en la presente y
sus ... con capa del secreto y religion; y porque venga a noticia ... de todos. Digo que
... el año de quarenta y tres, a Domingo de ... que fue de ... segun consta por ...
este tribunal y ... en mis descargos consta a todos los demas que son y fueron complices y caußas de mis agra...
y ... muerte, como consta de mi prisso de mi letra y mano fecha en el ... ... de Febrero del año de quarenta y ...
... sido vno ..., y principal autor el arcediano de Mexico Don Juan de Mañozca con ...
fue de ... que no solo ocultó los ... innumerables de los ... sino que cometio con ellos los mismos ...
... y otros, estando ... en poder de sus almas enemigos que son Juezes y parte, ...
y imposibilitando que no declaraßen los ... amancebados y ... y mas ...
... de visita que para ... cosas ... como Dios y ...
... con pretexto del secreto y religion; y porque de todas ...
... a dios que esta mi ... y yo las padezco mal, que no ... defiendo yo la ...
... con ... pero que ... por ... no me ... el otro ...
... no los condeno en las penas de muerte y ... que ... merecido, y antes ...
... y abrogacion de privilegios, que me guardaua antes ...
... y andamos ... con los ... ...
... ...

AN IRISH REBEL IN NEW SPAIN

The Tumultuous Life and Tragic Death of William Lamport

Andrea Martínez Baracs
Translated from the Spanish by Hank Heifetz

The Pennsylvania State University Press
University Park, Pennsylvania

Frontispiece First page of the "Proclamation of the Just Judgments of God."
AGN, vol. 1497, file 1, fol. 8r.

Library of Congress Cataloging-in-Publication Data

Names: Martínez Baracs, Andrea, author. | Lombardo, Guillén, 1615–1659,
  author. | Heifetz, Hank, translator.
Title: An Irish rebel in New Spain : the tumultuous life and tragic death
  of William Lamport / Andrea Martínez Baracs ; translated from the
  Spanish by Hank Heifetz.
Other titles: Don Guillén de Lampart, hijo de sus hazañas. English | Latin
  American originals ; 17.
Description: University Park, Pennsylvania : The Pennsylvania State
  University Press, [2021] | Series: Latin American originals ; 17 |
  Translation and revision of: Don Guillén de Lampart, hijo de sus
  hazañas, originally published in 2012. | Includes bibliographical
  references and index.
Summary: "Examines the life and work of William Lamport (d. 1659),
  an Irish rebel, soldier, poet, and thinker who was burned at the stake
  by the Inquisition in Mexico. Includes a collection of Lamport's most
  representative writings, including poetry, psalms, and a plan for a
  Mexican uprising against Spain"—Provided by publisher.
Identifiers: LCCN 2021037442 | ISBN 9780271090405 (paperback)
Subjects: LCSH: Lombardo, Guillén, 1615–1659. | Inquisition—Mexico—
  History—17th century. | Crypto-Jews—Mexico—History—17th
  century. | Manuscripts, Spanish—Mexico—Facsimiles. | Mexico—
  History—Spanish colony, 1540–1810.
Classification: LCC F1231.L843 M3713 2021 | DDC 972/.02—dc23
LC record available at https://lccn.loc.gov/2021037442

Published by The Pennsylvania State University Press,
University Park, PA 16802–1003

The Pennsylvania State University Press is a member of the Association of
University Presses.

It is the policy of The Pennsylvania State University Press to use acid-free
paper. Publications on uncoated stock satisfy the minimum requirements
of American National Standard for Information Sciences—Permanence of
Paper for Printed Library Material, ANSI Z39.48-1992.

CONTENTS

ILLUSTRATIONS

Latin American Originals (LAO) is a series of primary-source texts on colonial Latin America. LAO volumes are accessible editions of texts translated into English—most of them for the very first time. Of the seventeen volumes now in print, nine illuminate aspects of the Spanish invasions in the Americas during the long century of 1494–1614. The others take the series in varied and exciting directions, from the so-called spiritual conquest to medical science; the present volume also acts as a bridge between the invasion-era volumes and those exploring the mid- and late colonial periods.

Taken in the chronological order of their primary texts, *Of Cannibals and Kings* (LAO 7) comes first. It presents the earliest written attempts to describe Native American cultures, offering striking insight into how the first Europeans in the Americas struggled from the very start to conceive a "New World." *The Native Conquistador* (LAO 10) tells the story of the (in)famous Spanish Conquest expeditions into Mexico and Central America from 1519 to 1524—but from the startlingly different perspective of an Indigenous dynasty, with Ixtlilxochitl, ruler of Tetzcoco, the alternative leading protagonist, as recounted by his great-great-grandson.

Next, chronologically, are LAOs 2, 1, and 9. *Invading Guatemala* shows how reading multiple accounts of conquest wars (in this case, Spanish, Nahua, and Maya versions of the Guatemalan conflict of the 1520s) can explode established narratives and suggest a more complex and revealing conquest story. *Invading Colombia* challenges us to view the difficult Spanish invasion of Colombia in the 1530s as more representative of conquest campaigns than the better-known assaults on the Aztec and Inca Empires. It complements *The Improbable Conquest*, which presents letters written between 1537 and 1556 by Spaniards struggling—with a persistence that is improbable indeed—to plant a colony along the hopefully named Río de la Plata.

Contesting Conquest (LAO 12) adds intriguingly to that trio, offering new perspectives on Nueva Galicia's understudied early history. Indigenous witnesses and informants, their voices deftly identified, selected, and presented, guide us through the grim, messy tale of repeated efforts at conquest and colonization from the late 1520s through 1545.

LAOs 11, 3, 4, and 16 all explore aspects of the aftermath and legacy of the invasion era. *The History of the New World* offers the first English translation since 1847 of part of a 1565 Italian book that, in its day, was a best seller in five languages. The merchant-adventurer Girolamo Benzoni mixed sharp observations and sympathy for Indigenous peoples with imaginary tales and wild history, influencing generations of early modern readers and challenging modern readers to sort out fact from fable. *The Conquest on Trial* features a fictional Indigenous embassy filing a complaint over in a court in Spain—the Court of Death. The first theatrical examination of the conquest published in Spain, it effectively condensed contemporary debates on colonization into one dramatic package. It contrasts well with *Defending the Conquest*, which presents a spirited, ill-humored, and polemic apologia for the Spanish Conquest, written in 1613 by a veteran conquistador.

LAO 16 takes us from Italian and Spanish perspectives on early colonization to those of a Nahua family. Viewed through their own Nahuatl-language papers, *Indigenous Life After the Conquest* shows how the family navigated the gradual changes and challenges that swept central Mexico in the century after the upheaval of invasion— as a new order was built, contested, and shaped by Nahuas themselves.

LAO 16 dovetails in many ways with volumes 13, 6, 5, and 8— which explore aspects of Spanish efforts to implant Christianity in the Americas. Chronologically, *To Heaven or to Hell* leads the pack, presenting the first complete English translation of a book by Bartolomé de Las Casas. Originally published in 1552, his *Confessionary for Confessors*—soon overshadowed by his famous *Very Brief Account of the Destruction of the Indies*—was initially just as controversial; conquistadors and other Spaniards were outraged by its demand that they themselves be subjected to spiritual conquest imperatives.

Gods of the Andes presents the first English edition of a 1594 manuscript describing Inca religion and the campaign to convert native Andeans. Its Jesuit author is surprisingly sympathetic to preconquest beliefs and practices, viewing them as preparing Andeans for the arrival of the new faith. *Forgotten Franciscans* casts new light on the conflictive cultural world of the Inquisition in sixteenth-century Mexico. Both LAO 6 and 5 expose wildly divergent views within the Spanish American church on native religions and how to replace them with Christianity. Complementing those two volumes by revealing the Indigenous side to the same process, *Translated Christianities* presents religious texts translated from Nahuatl and Yucatec Maya. Designed to proselytize and ensure the piety of Indigenous parishioners, these texts show how such efforts actually contributed to the development of local Christianities.

The present volume, LAO 17, takes the series into the seventeenth century, casting a sharp eye on the far-reaching intrigues of colonial and inquisitorial politics. *An Irish Rebel in New Spain* explores the life and writings of William Lamport, an Irishman who rose through colonial Mexican society only to lose his life in the clutches of the Holy Office. This volume presents Lamport's unique writings, theological philosophies, and damning critiques of the legal workings of the Inquisition. The life and literary efforts of the Irish Zorro, as he was called, are the means whereby highly respected and accomplished Mexican scholar Andrea Martínez Baracs sheds light on the cruel whimsy of (mis)fortune in a time of upheaval and instability in Spanish America.

LAOs 14 and 15 push the series further still into new territory. *To the Shores of Chile* presents the "Journal and History" of a Dutch expedition to Chile, bringing to more than seven the number of languages from which LAO sources have been translated. Extending the series into a new region of the Americas, it opens up a novel perspective on European-Indigenous interaction, colonization, and global competition in the age of empire. *Baptism Through Incision* takes the series later in time and into medical history, using an eighteenth-century Guatemalan case study to explore the fascinating intersections between faith and science in the early modern world. This first English publication and presentation of an eye-opening 1786 treatise on performing cesareans on pregnant women at the moment of their death explores anew many of the themes that are threaded through previous volumes—empire, salvation, the female body, and knowledge as a battleground.

The source texts in LAO volumes are colonial-era rare books or archival documents, written in European or Mesoamerican languages. LAO authors are historians, anthropologists, art historians, geographers, and scholars of literature who have developed a specialized knowledge that allows them to locate, translate, and present these texts in a way that contributes to scholars' understanding of the period, while also making them readable for students and nonspecialists. Martínez Baracs is just such a scholar, uniquely qualified to enhance the series with her skills and insights.

—Matthew Restall

ACKNOWLEDGMENTS

This English-language edition, a revised and enriched version of the Spanish-language edition with three added sets of documents, was made possible by the support of the Irish embassy in Mexico, the Mexican embassy in Ireland, and Emilio Pimentel, from Dallas, Texas.

Introduction

And I answered him, "Then the sacred Catholic faith teaches this kind of murder?"
And they remained silent, as representatives of severe divinity.
—William Lamport

Engulfed in the Storm

There are historical personages whose lives absorb and connect many histories, who manage to epitomize their age, becoming the intersection of currents stemming from very distant sources. William Lamport was one such person. Born in either 1611 or 1615 and living until 1659, he was an Irish Catholic soldier and a dedicated supporter of the rebellion against the English led by the Earl of Tyrone from 1593 to 1603. Lamport was a theologian, astrologer, grammarian, mathematician, rhetorician, poet, courtier, and conspirator during the first half of the seventeenth century, when the Spanish monarchy was involved in the double task of retaining its empire and regaining its former power. He was an intrepid member of the Spanish army's Irish regiments in its European wars, a rebel in Ireland and Mexico, and a valiant but ill-fated adventurer who fell foul of the Inquisition in New Spain, to which both the pope and the king of Spain were to appeal in his favor.

Not only did Lamport figure in various strands of history, but his exploits were numerous and often unfortunate. He arrived in New Spain in 1640, purportedly sent in secret by the king's counselor and favorite, the Count-Duke of Olivares. The 1638 Catalan revolt was fresh in the memory, and Spain had also failed to retake the seacoast

FIG. 1 William Lamport's coat of arms, as elaborated by himself. ITESM, fol. 206v.

of Brazil from the Dutch. The intrigues and uprisings that would lead to Portugal's ultimately successful rebellion against Spain (which broke out on December 1, 1640) were in full swing. It was, in all, a year of crisis for the Spanish Crown and its dominions, with the country on the verge of bankruptcy. It was a moment when it seemed that anything might happen.

William Lamport traveled to New Spain in the same ship as the two most important figures in the affairs of New Spain at the time: the newly appointed viceroy, the Marquis of Villena and Duke of Escalona, and Juan de Palafox y Mendoza, the royal inspector for New Spain and resident judge for the tenure of the viceroyalty. Lamport was twenty-five or twenty-nine when he first set foot in Mexico in 1640, a year of signal political and social turmoil there as well. Royal inspector and resident judge Juan de Palafox would later (in June 1642) strip the Marquis of Villena of his title on charges of corruption and suspected collusion with Portugal, in spite of the marquis's position as a grandee of Spain. Palafox, during his nine years in New Spain, served mainly as the bishop of Puebla, but he was at different times also appointed royal inspector and resident judge. As such, he investigated the tenures of a series of viceroys and would himself briefly fill the posts of viceroy and archbishop of Mexico. He also launched relentless assaults on the prerogatives of both the Franciscans and Jesuits. Meanwhile, the serious loss of territory suffered by the Spanish Crown was accompanied by the resounding collapse of certain political careers, in particular that of the count-duke, who had held considerable power and been Lamport's protector; he was abruptly removed from office in 1643, shortly after Lamport's imprisonment in New Spain. Lamport thought himself in the eye of the hurricane, only to be engulfed by the storm.

An avid student of the courts of Europe, where palace intrigues and international politics of the highest level met, Lamport, intensely aware of the maneuvering of a profusion of nobles and functionaries, governors, potentates, and the pope himself, arrived in New Spain at the time of Portugal's violent secession from the Spanish Crown. Portugal's breakaway led directly to an intensified persecution of crypto-Jews (*marranos*) in Spanish territories. Expelled from Spain in 1492 by Queen Isabel I, many had fled to Portugal, in particular during the decades when it was not under Spanish rule. When Spain reannexed Portugal in 1580, many of these families (having now become Portuguese subjects and taken Portuguese names) emigrated back to Spain and to the Americas, where they rose, particularly through the trading of slaves and textiles, to distinguished positions in the commercial and financial world. Through innovations and a huge network of contacts and partners, in the 1600s they were responsible for underwriting the vast array of Spanish commercial ventures in the Philippines, China, and India, through Mexico and the other American territories to Cádiz and all of Europe. The Count-Duke of Olivares and Lamport himself were in favor of protecting these Portuguese crypto-Jewish financiers who were being persecuted by the Inquisition, since their resources promised to save the Spanish Crown (and the count-duke himself) from bankruptcy precipitated by the wars in Europe.

As a real or supposed secret agent of the Count-Duke of Olivares—I have found no definitive proof either way—Lamport concerned himself with the gathering of reports and rumors concerning possible separatist intrigues, the Crown's greatest worry at that time. The Marquis of Villena was cousin to the Duke of Braganza, the separatist Portuguese king, and a number of glaring missteps on the marquis's part had led the king of Spain to doubt his loyalty. He would be stripped of his office with no prior notice and removed from his position as viceroy largely due to a secret report on his activities, a report that has been attributed to Lamport and might very well be his work. The marquis swore vengeance and may have gone on to be the architect of Lamport's own fall from grace.

How did Lamport go about conveying secret information in a time when unconditional allegiance to those in power was nonnegotiable and informers everywhere were quick to whisper accusations? Two years after his arrival in New Spain, Lamport made the error of trying to pass a confidential letter through people connected to the Inquisition. Denounced on the morning of Sunday, October 26, 1642, he was arrested by the Holy Office that same night. He was imprisoned for seventeen years, though he managed to escape, for only a few hours, on Christmas 1650. At the time of his escape, an Inquisition edict described him as a "man of medium stature, with a red beard and hair tending toward chestnut in color, of lean build, pallid of complexion, with very lively eyes."[1] While awaiting trial by the Holy Office, Lamport spent his time making denunciations of his own, denying the many charges laid against him and denouncing the venality, lack of scruples, illegality, and flawed faith in those who would be his executioners. He was burned alive (though he may have succeeded in killing himself moments before the flames reached his body) in the auto-da-fé of November 19, 1659, in Mexico City. The edict issued to justify the final sentence is as follows:

> [Lamport] was declared a sectarian heretic who partook of the heresies of Calvin, Pelagius, Jan Hus, Wycliffe, and Luther and of the Illuminati and other heresiarchs; a dogmatist; an inventor of new heresies; an instigator; and defender of heresies, obstinate and persistent, and for these reasons having fallen into and incurred a sentence of major excommunication and being linked to this judgment [and hence] to the confiscation and loss of all the possessions that in any way belong to him, which [seizure of possessions] we order to be carried out and [for this purpose] we apply to the assembly and royal treasury of this Inquisition.[2]

Academic and Soldier

In the long history of Ireland, there has been no lack of learned soldiers or careers forged outside the country. William Lamport, born, according to his brother, on February 25, 1611 (in 1615, according to Lamport himself), and an expatriate from a young age, had both a brilliant academic career and a military career of some distinction. During his long imprisonment he would write about both careers, in

1. "Traslado de los autos fulminados contra Don Guillen Lombardo (alias) Guillermo Lampart presso en las cárceles secretas de este Santo Oficio desde el día que hizo fuga de dichas cárceles y buelta a ellas," Archivo Histórico Nacional (hereafter cited as AHN), Madrid, Inquisición, Tribunal de México, Procesos de Fe, Guillen Lombardo de Guzmán, Diego Pinto y Luis de Olivera, 1650, file 1731-4/53, no. 24, fols. 29r–29v.
2. The complete sentence is reproduced at the end of the second volume of the novel by Riva Palacio: *Memorias de un impostor*. This final extract is on pages 343–44.

detail and occasionally with some exaggeration. The psychological and moral debasement of life in the Inquisition dungeons throws a certain apparently fraudulent patina over his narrative; some of the exploits to which he lays claim seem quite incredible. Nevertheless, discounting rhetorical exaggerations and some white lies not uncommon in such an account in those days, plus a febrile style also not so surprising given the circumstances of his captivity, the historical record supports his assertions. The basic facts of his autobiography are genuine, as I myself discovered in the process of gathering evidence and as established by his diligent biographer, the Italian historian Fabio Troncarelli.

His family, originally Norman, came from the lesser nobility of Wexford and included a number of soldiers. He was given a Jesuit education and afterward sent to study in London. Sometime between 1626 and 1628, his father was accused of conspiring with the Spaniards and, abandoning his activities and his fortune, took refuge in a monastery, perhaps for the rest of his life. A few years later Lamport cut short his academic career by publishing a short poem (now lost) criticizing the king of England. It was 1628 and he was seventeen (or thirteen) years old. He claims that he had written "a book in elegant Latin in defense of our faith against the power of a king. . . . Having grown up in the court of England, where my teacher was Father Batheo of the Society of Jesus, I wrote a book at ten years of age entitled *Defenso fidei contra Carolum Anglia Regum*, the translation of which is in the royal library of His Majesty in San Lorenzo."[3] He was condemned to death and had to flee from England, never to return. The fugitive boarded a boat headed for the continent, but the ship was captured by pirates. Lamport remained at sea for two years and, when they finally came into port, claimed to have converted the entire crew. According to Troncarelli, this was not an impossible claim. The conversion could have been a deception designed to free his shipmate pirates and already marks Lamport as an intrepid man, an academic not lacking in courage or love of adventure.

And so he arrived in Spain, first (1631–32) at the Jesuit college of San Patricio (Saint Patrick, the patron saint of Ireland) at Santiago de Galicia, which was populated with Irishmen because of its proximity to southern Ireland across the sea. There he received a scholarship

---

3. "Traslado de los autos fulminados," AHN, no. 24, fols. 13v–14v, 185v–186r.

to continue his studies. He went on to the Irish college of Salamanca and from there to a private university for the sons of court nobles. When his scholarship funds ran out, his patron, the count-duke, sent him to accompany the brother of the king, Cardinal-Infante Ferdinand of Austria, in Spain's European wars. From 1633 to 1635, at the head of a unit of Irishmen, Lamport fought for Spain, notably in Bavaria at the 1634 battle of Nördlingen. He took part in the famous battle of Fuenterrabía (now Hondarribia in Spain). The description of his military campaigns, written in his prison declarations, is supported by the historical records:

> I proceeded to Flanders in the company of His Highness Cardinal-Infante. . . . I organized the squadrons of Norlenghen [Nördlingen] according to a new mathematical scheme. . . . I fought in the relief of Lobayna. I brought, in a brief time, the messages of His Majesty to Venice. I participated with noteworthy valor in the bloody battle of the English Channel, twenty-five galleons confronting fifty, and two rebel galleons entering Donhencon. . . . I joined with two hundred Catholics in the first stage of assistance to Domingo de Eguía in Fuenteravia [Fuenterrabía] . . . and I did all this before I had reached twenty-three years of age.[4]

Upon his return, his reputation made now due to his martial exploits, he became a student again at Colegio del Escorial at San Lorenzo, where he had access to the court and the richly compendious library of the monastery.[5] Here is a summary of his educational and academic studies, as he recounted to his inquisitors in their first formal interrogation after his arrest:

> At six years of age, I was entrusted to the university graduate Guillermo de Verox, a saintly man and high functionary of the church, vicar general of the Ferns diocese, and a resident of my father's city, who in turn entrusted me to Father Thomas

---

4. Ibid.
5. There exists a report that the library of the monastery of El Escorial in 1639 possessed 932 prohibited books, which is highly unusual (Kamen, *Spanish Inquisition*). Very likely it held the translation of Lamport's own *Defenso fidei*, as he claimed.

Furlong of the Augustinian order to teach me how to read and write and also to learn grammar. Then I had, as teachers of Latin poesy, Fathers Antonio Tornero and Gualtero Chepero, then Fathers Thomas Quinn and Henry Plunkett of the Society of Jesus as teachers of Latin rhetoric at the court of Ireland. At the court of London, I had the Jesuit father Batheo as a teacher in celestial and world geometry and Master Gray in natural magic. In Spain the rest of my teachers were Father Ildefonso de Amaya of the Society of Jesus in metaphysical philosophy and logic, Dr. Roales (also the teacher of the lord infante-cardinal) in astrology, and in sacred theology the father-teachers of Father Juan de Toledo and Father Miguel de Santa María of the Order of Saint Jerome. And also in the study of fortifications and squadrons, the Jesuit father Gamaso, an Italian; and in optics and hydraulics Father Claudio Ricardo, a Burgundian. In geography, hydrography, and nautical science, Father Falla, a Fleming and a Jesuit; in hourly astrology and the secrets of nature, Father Eusebio de Noremberge, a Fleming and a Jesuit; in mathematics and numerical geometry, the Jesuit father Ysasi, a Biscayan; in politics the Jesuit father Poza, who also had [direct] experience in these miseries.

He also studied, he added, "secret matters of state," the Greek language, alchemy, the art of memory, chemistry, architecture, secret philosophy, and sacred scripture.[6] The list testifies to the rich, multinational, cultural tradition furthered by the Spanish monarchy and the Jesuit education of the time. One of Lamport's great teachers was the famous and deeply learned Jesuit Juan Eusebio Nieremberg. He was a neo-Stoic and author of the book *Historia naturae, maxime peregrinae* (published in 1635). His work is related to that of the extraordinary Jesuit scholar Athanasius Kircher, devoted to the study of nature and natural magic. Nieremberg was a close friend of Juan de Palafox, who preached an austere morality and argued the case of the idealistic knight, incorruptible and willing to stand alone against evil. He was one of the favorite authors of the Mexican scholar Don Carlos de Sigüenza y Góngora (1645–1700).

6. "Traslado de los autos fulminados," AHN, no. 24, fols. 49v–50r.

During William Lamport's university years, the young men of the Spanish court were passionately involved in the ideas of the rebels within the church, like the Jesuit Juan Baptista Poza, a "verbose and acclaimed" orator, deprived of office in 1623 and stubbornly resistant to the edict against him, and, as Lamport said with elegant understatement, "who also had [direct] experience in these miseries."[7] Troncarelli asserts that he influenced Lamport, and clearly their modes of behavior and their very careers resembled each other. But the most outstanding example of this trend at that time was the Spanish Jesuit Juan de Mariana, celebrated author of *De rege et regis institutione*, where he glorified the act of tyrannicide. He was condemned by the priestly council of the Sorbonne, which triggered an enormous scandal. De Mariana emerged unscathed and continued to fight for his ideas. He wrote with ferocity despite censure by the head of his order. He died in 1644, and his ideas were discussed in secret and his indomitable pride admired. From such courage and audacity rose the image of what Troncarelli terms a "heroic ideal of Christian militancy" for the young men of the Spanish court.[8] The life led by Lamport, including his martyrdom in New Spain, was surely a match for the examples of his teachers.

An Irish Revolutionary of an Ancient Lineage

The revolutionary passion that William Lamport rediscovered in New Spain stemmed from his Irish origins. Before arriving in Mexico in 1640, he participated in the secret planning of a rebellion against the English in Ireland. Because of his ties with important personages in the Spanish court, especially the Count-Duke of Olivares, King Philip IV's favorite, he was well placed to help in the process of negotiating international support—diplomatic, financial, and military— for the impending Irish Rebellion.

Planned in secret to be launched on October 23, 1641—on the day honoring Saint Ignatius of Loyola—the rebellion sought to take advantage of the Scottish Rising against Charles I and the English Parliament's refusal to submit to their king. In England as well, the

7. Ibid., fol. 192v.
8. Troncarelli, *Spada e la croce*.

world seemed to be falling apart. The plans for the insurrection, however, were betrayed and what might have been a relatively peaceful seizure of power was brutally stifled by the English army. The resultant rising of the Irish populace against the English and Scottish colonists was terribly cruel and bloody on both sides. Even today the Protestants of the Orange Order and the Irish Catholics talk of the massacres of 1641. The English Parliament passed the Adventurer's Act, which, in March 1642, promised land grants in Ireland to speculators or mercenaries who could assemble armies to attack the Irish. Lamport, away in New Spain, may have heard little about this, but whatever distressing news reached him must have been more than sufficient.

Fabio Troncarelli affirms that, in 1639, shortly before he left for New Spain, Lamport had obtained 42,000 ducats from the count-duke to facilitate preparations for the uprising. There also existed, says Troncarelli, a royal authorization that assigned him the explicit mission of recruiting troops for Ireland. Various Irish Franciscan friars were purportedly also involved in this project, beginning with Lamport's own brother, Father Juan Lombardo. According to Troncarelli, the connection between Lamport and Bishop Palafox included a joint concern with the Irish project, and men acting in the name of Palafox helped Lamport with his brief escape from prison in 1650. As yet I have not found documented corroboration of these assertions.

Among Lamport's private papers in the Colección Conway of the Instituto Tecnológico y de Estudios Superiores de Monterrey (ITESM) is a detailed plan, in Lamport's own handwriting, to convert Ireland into a protectorate of Spain, united to the Crown as a free republic, provided the king would closely involve Spain in the Irish insurrection. This petition has been attributed to Gilbert Nugent, the informal ambassador to the court of Spain for the many Irish earls willing to fight against the English domination of their country. The proposal in Lamport's handwriting, which we are publishing here, is a copy of such a petition, and Lamport may have been its coauthor.

Lamport was the son and grandson of soldiers who fought in the great Irish Rebellion of 1593 to 1603, Tyrone's Rebellion—English historians gave this name to the rebellion, which among the Irish is known as the Nine Years' War. Lamport says that his father "conveyed, with his fleet of ships, the troops of His Majesty, in order to help the lord prince of Tyrone and Tyrconnel . . . and in the course of fifteen years my grandfather and father with their armies put more than one hundred thousand enemies to the sword, capturing two English viceroys in battles."[9]

The life story of Hugh O'Neill, Earl of Tyrone, a man committed to palace intrigues, has certain resemblances with that of Lamport. Protected in his childhood and youth by Queen Elizabeth of England, he returned to Ireland in 1595, turned against the queen, and was dubbed the "traitor earl." His rebellion was the last and greatest of the Elizabethan rebellions against English colonialism in Ireland. His defeat at the Battle of Kinsale in 1602 marked the end of Gaelic government and the submission of all Ireland. The leaders of the uprising, for their part, joined the Flight of the Earls, a filmic escape of ninety-nine Irish warriors and nobles on board a ship that took them to mainland Europe. The exile of the Earl Hugh (Aedh in Gaelic) lasted from 1602 to 1616. He traveled to Rome, where he lived out his life through the grace of the pope and the king of Spain.

Beginning in 1603, England subjected Ireland to the so-called policy of plantations (officially known as the "plantation of Ulster"), which displaced the native Irish in favor of English and Scottish colonists, who were then forbidden to intermarry with Irish women. The Irish lost rights to their land and were made to rent their former properties. Catholics were persecuted and could practice their religion only as a clandestine cult. Under Charles I all the land in North Wexford, including the dwellings of the Lamports, was assigned to the English Crown by means of some legal fabrications. Only 350 native Irishmen were given the status of legal landholders, while 14,500 remained on their land at the mercy of Protestant English or Scottish. Tensions grew until flaring up into the Irish rising of 1641.

Philip III supported the Irish Catholics against Queen Elizabeth, and, after the failure of the uprising, a sizable number of them arrived in Spain. The Old Irish Division, commanded by the Earl of Tyrone, took part in a number of campaigns in Flanders and afterward fought in the 1638 Catalan revolt. They continued to serve the Spanish monarchy until, in 1681, the unit dissolved following the death of Brian Roe O'Neill, a late inheritor of the earldom of Tyrone.

From 1631 to 1641 the Irish diaspora (to which Lamport belonged) and the oppressed Catholics of Ireland were in constant

9. Lombardo, *Cristiano desagravio y retractaciones*, 45.

communication. From 1632 on the Spaniards were authorized to recruit soldiers in Ireland. Owen Roe O'Neill, a nephew of Hugh O'Neill, was for a period of twenty-five years a sergeant major and then a captain in the Eighty Years' War.[10] He was a major leader of the Irish uprising of 1642–49 and took charge of recruiting among the clans. He dedicated himself to organizing the Irish into a great military brotherhood, committed to conspiracies and intrigues. Other leaders included Thomas Tyrell of County Westmeath and Thomas Preston. John, the last surviving son of the Earl of Tyrone, would die in battle in Catalonia.

In the north of Ireland, the Irish Rebellion of 1641 was led by Sir Phelim O'Neill. Among his exploits was the publication of a falsified document that claimed the king of Spain had authorized the rebellion, the kind of conspiratorial move Lamport would also make. (As we have mentioned, Lamport was instrumental in the fomenting of this important uprising, acting as a more international version of the O'Neills.)[11]

For Lamport the liberation of New Spain could be compared to the hoped-for liberation of Ireland. In both cases ancient rights had been stripped from the native inhabitants, to whom the land truly belonged. And in both cases he threw himself headfirst into his plans for liberation. For that reason, seeing himself, in his own words, as the "offspring of [his] own exploits," he felt that he justly merited recognition by the liberated *naturales*, or natives, as their "prince and king." Coexisting in Lamport's mind were two insurrectional, but strikingly different, projects. The first offered the king of Spain the chance to convert Ireland into a protectorate—and, ironically, to introduce the Inquisition into that country!—while, in his proposal for an uprising in New Spain, his plan was to split New Spain from

10. Owen Roe O'Neill was one of the ninety-nine fugitives in the Flight of the Earls. He was raised in the Spanish Low Countries and served for twenty-five years in the Irish regiment of the Spanish army.

11. The Ulster Rebellion of 1641 went on until the Irish rebels were defeated by Oliver Cromwell's army in 1649. It had succeeded in annihilating the principal Irish Protestant army and threatened the English domination of Ireland. It was extremely bloody. It is estimated that twelve thousand Protestants died, in battle or from massacres, of a total Protestant population of forty thousand. The final massacres of the Irish rebels were of the same magnitude, and certainly one of the most notorious massacres took place in County Wexford, where Lamport was born. See "English and Scottish Planters."

the Spanish Crown through rebellion. According to Lamport's arguments, both projects were justified (and coincided) because they were responses to illegal domination. One would think that the persuasive power of Lamport's proposal for Ireland would be damaged by the disloyalty shown in this project. In any case, the Irish uprising was launched, and it did not receive any direct involvement from the Spanish Crown. The defeated Irish, the "Wild Geese," flocked over the course of the century to the king of Spain, under whose orders his Irish divisions were formed.[12]

"They Are All First-Rate Thieves"

The reign of Philip IV was defined by his intense warmongering against the Protestant world, of which Amsterdam was a great representative: a port open to the world and to free trade, to the circulation of goods and ideas and the rise of the bourgeoisie.[13] Rejecting his enemy's example completely, he embraced and further stymied the progress of a society that was already profoundly corrupted and economically dysfunctional. The corruption, indifference, and cynicism of the officials entrusted with the Inquisition in New Spain would be made all too clear through William Lamport's case; during his seventeen years' captivity, he would expose and denounce those officials in a systematic and exhaustive way. Far from yielding to them or being weakened by his daily round of suffering within prison, this "culprit" dedicated himself to registering the abuses and aberrations not only against himself but against his fellow prisoners.

The true motive for Lamport's arrest was the case he made to the king (in his intercepted letter) concerning the fraudulent logic behind the persecution of the Portuguese crypto-Jews in New Spain. In one of his accusations, which he nailed to the doors of the Metropolitan

---

12. Stradling, *Spanish Monarchy*. The tumultuous history of the Irish in the seventeenth century is well documented.

13. "They are all first-rate thieves" is a statement of Don Bernardo Guerrero, a Portuguese convert and lawyer connected with the Audiencia de México. Guerrero was arrested on the strength of this statement, which made reference to the same inquisitors who persecuted William Lamport (Inquisición, vol. 429, fols. 406r, 406v, quoted in Israel, *Empires and Entrepôts*, 323).

Cathedral and delivered to the viceroy during his brief hours of freedom in 1650, he reformulated the arguments from the letter:

> The Inquisition found a clause written for the purpose of reminding Your Majesty, and it stated that they had in this city, under the cover of [charges of] Judaism, arrested sixty families who were among the most powerful in the kingdom. That if it were true that they were listed [as "Judaizers"] Your Majesty should order that this should then be dealt with, less [the inquisitors] consume the impounded wealth, under the pretext of [necessary] delays, because there was a great sum [available] for very badly needed assistance [to the Crown], and if [these families] were not listed, then the same problem [would arise], because they [the inquisitors] would be destroying commerce and vassals and dependents with serious damage to [your] royal rights.

Elsewhere, referring to a major crypto-Jewish financier of New Spain, he writes, "They have arrested a man named Simón Váez . . . and with this one action they have swallowed up, in an instant, more than 500,000 pesos belonging to him and to others."[14]

Lamport met the victims in the jail. The auto-da-fé on Saturday, April 10, 1649, in Mexico City's Plaza de Volador was the primary blow against the great crypto-Jewish financiers and merchants and their families. Thirteen people were burned alive: six women and seven men. Twenty-seven other people, including Simón Váez and a number of his relatives, were sentenced to two hundred lashes, delivered on that day. Sixty-six statues of men and women, representations of deceased persons as well as coffins containing the bones of others—at least ten had died in the jails of the Inquisition—were carried away on the backs of Indians and burned as well. Most of these were newly converted Christians accused of continuing to practice Judaism in secret. Most of these "Judaizers," both those who were executed and those whose lives were spared, and all their offspring too, had all of their possessions confiscated.

14. "Traslado de los autos fulminados," AHN, no. 24, fols. 9v, 96r. I am greatly indebted to Silvia E. Aguilera Noriega and Zoraida G. Ríos Morales for transcribing this long and difficult file.

The Inquisition, founded as an ecclesiastical tribunal under the authority of the state in New Spain in 1569–71, did not have a formal financial basis of its own. Salaries were paid from the proceeds of fines and confiscations, above all, confiscations of the wealth of heretics (canon law dictated that their possessions had to be seized), the persecution of whom was therefore principally a matter of raising money.[15] Plundering the fortunes of the great crypto-Jewish converts (*conversos*) financiers of New Spain brought abundant wealth, fortunes worth many millions of ducats, directly into the hands of the inquisitors, much of it going from there into their pockets. The money was supposed to pay for the costs of the tribunal, with most of it to be sent directly to the Supreme Council of the Inquisition of Spain. But, shielded by their impunity, the inquisitors developed all sorts of methods for personally appropriating the wealth of their prisoners.

The corruption reached a peak in Lamport's time in jail but was followed by a series of royal actions that sought to tackle it by replacing most of the officials in charge of the Inquisition's tribunal. One may assume that Lamport's denunciations came to the attention of the bishop of Puebla, Juan de Palafox, the great reformer, and were thus at the basis of this partial rectification. If so, his sacrifice was not entirely in vain.

First came the formal Royal Inspection of the tribunal, initiated in 1645 (very similar to present-day audits concerned with finances but also an examination of civil matters and issues particular to the Holy Office).[16] The first inspector was Archbishop Juan de Mañozca, who was an uncle of the venal inquisitor of the same name, Juan Sáenz de Mañozca. He seemed unlikely to take his investigations very far or would at least seek to protect his relative. Nevertheless, the inquisitor Domingo Vélez de Assas y Argos, the personal persecutor of Lamport in his jail, was suspended from office in 1647, and a prosecutor was also excommunicated. Amid growing scandal the archbishop would finally resign his position as inspector for the Holy Inquisition.

The new inspector was Don Pedro de Medina Rico, who had been sent simultaneously to inspect affairs in Cartagena de Indias. He commenced his duties in 1651, two years after the auto-da-fé of

---

15. Kamen, *Spanish Inquisition*.
16. Medina, *Historia del Tribunal*, 211–17, 221–66.

1649. A surprising number of legal cases (around 1,200) were in process against the fiscal arm of the Inquisition's tribunal in New Spain. All the inquisitors, without exception, were convicted, having been found guilty of a huge number of offenses, from the illegal appropriation of goods intended for the Treasury, down to cruel mistreatment of prisoners. (Against Francisco de Estrada y Escobedo alone there were 111 charges; against Sáenz de Mañozca, eighteen entire chapters of accusations.) The sentence was delivered in May 1662. None were exonerated. Medina Rico also denounced the conditions of the prisons of the Holy Office and wanted to improve them. The prisons were collapsing and had been flooded during the rainy season, so in winter they were uninhabitable "because of the cold in those days. Moreover, the cots where the prisoners slept and the bedclothes given to the poor who had to sleep on the floor were all rotted." In spite of his plea, nothing was repaired or remedied.[17]

A Rebel in New Spain

The hundreds of pages of documents from William Lamport's trial makes it clear that the real motive for his arrest was to prevent his secret reports from reaching Madrid. The Inquisition itself, precisely the institution that arrested him, was the major object of his accusations. To nullify him they accused him of various heresies, including the use of the hallucinogenic cactus peyote for the purpose of divination and the application of black magic (supposedly to cure impotence, including the conjuring of an apparition "in the form of a dog or a cat"). He was also accused of "judiciary astrology," which, according to ecclesiastical dogma, clashed with the doctrine of free will upheld by the church. Lamport clearly understood the trap and disassembled it piece by piece.[18] Theologian that he was, he explained in depth how these attempts to tarnish his credentials as a believer were in themselves assaults on the faith. The defense he mounted is a theological treatise and at the same time (as anyone reading these papers will quickly discover) a hurricane of anger.

17. Ibid., 264.
18. Lombardo, *Cristiano desagravio y retractaciones*, 85.

The unprecedented behavior of Lamport in prison and the power and gravity of his denunciations succeeded in reaching the highest powers in Europe. The king of Spain himself questioned the tribunal of the Inquisition, stained as it was by such serious and well-documented accusations. The king requested, in vain, that the prisoner be delivered to him, as well as the records of his trial.[19] The confrontation between the Crown and church even led the Vatican to try to intervene. The only plausible explanation for Lamport's brief escape in 1650 is that it was facilitated by an important figure, perhaps someone in the service of Bishop Juan de Palafox—although Palafox himself, by that time, had already left for Spain.[20]

There were, in a sense, many Lamports. One of them we have just seen, a rebel in good faith who describes a shameful and lamentable situation and denounces it without a thought for the possible personal consequences. Imprisoned, and completely alone, with no imaginable hope of assistance, he fought his accusations with the most notable reasoning and cogent arguments, demonstrated by the hundreds of pages of documents dating from the time of his incarceration (1642 to 1659).

But the imprisoned Lamport was also a poet in Latin, admired by the learned Mexican Gabriel Méndez Plancarte in words such as the following: "Despite twelve years enduring the harshest prison regimen, he wrote the coruscating and in a certain sense prophetic psalms, hymns in Sapphic-Adonic, and Asclepian-Glyconic strophes that show an almost perfect control of complicated Greco-Latin metrics and a by-no-means ordinary understanding of the classics."[21] But there is yet more to William Lamport, hidden away in his "small trunk from Michoacán": his personal archive, confiscated on the day

19. The dispute between the king of Spain and the Inquisition of New Spain over the case of William Lamport was already significant in 1643, grew more heated after his brief escape in 1650, and continued until at least 1667. It is clear that the Inquisition came out the winner. Cf. the letters, dating from 1650 to 1653, of the Viceroy Conde de Alba de Liste, in the Archivo General de Indias, Seville, file: México, 36, no. 54; and González Obregón, *D. Guillén de Lámport*, 233–35.

20. The Italian historian Fabio Troncarelli, author of an exhaustive investigation on William Lamport, states that Bishop Palafox was close to Lamport and even an accomplice in organizing the Irish revolt and in Lamport's plans for an uprising. Troncarelli, *Spada e la croce*. I have not yet found corroboration for these assertions.

21. Méndez Plancarte, *Don Guillén de Lámport*.

of his arrest and used in the proceedings against him.[22] These papers laid bare his intentions and led eventually to his downfall.

The most important revelations concerning his life before imprisonment are the following. He was a secret agent of the Count-Duke of Olivares. The Inquisition (as have many present-day historians) refused to accept Lamport's claim to this appointment, just as they have denied the truth of many of his exploits and personal achievements. But Troncarelli considers it a proven fact. Among the papers of the ITESM, there is a copy of a secret statement shared by Lamport and a secretary very close to the count-duke, with the secretary's signature. His personal papers also showed that he was an active agent of the imminent Irish Rebellion (something of little interest to the Inquisition's tribunal). In his proclamation of New Spain's independence, written by Lamport and included in the trunk, the Irishman declared that the papal concession of the Americas to the king of Spain was not legitimate.[23] After writing this grievous disloyalty to the king, he then elaborated a revolutionary and separatist project, unpardonable by the Crown at such a moment of threat to the integrity of the empire. But the element most emphasized by the Inquisition was his claim to a different identity. He alleges that he is an illegitimate son of the previous king, kept at a distance and never recognized, a claim that fills whole pages of the proclamation, which cannot be properly understood without attention to this more "personal" component. It was more than a rebel adopting a false identity; it aimed at converting the takeover of New Spain into a strictly personal issue: the bastard prince, an idealist tired of awaiting the recognition that his military exploits and brilliant academic credentials deserved, tries to rescue a kingdom, empowering slaves and natives and winning a new crown for himself. Is this an extreme case of egomania, of a knight errant trying to straddle the world? Yet

22. "Inventario de los papeles que se hallaron en un baúl pequeño de Mechoacán que al tiempo de la prisión se le cogió a Don Guillén Lombardo de Guzmán," Instituto Tecnológico y de Estudios Superiores de Monterrey (hereafter cited as ITESM), Biblioteca Cervantina, Patrimonio Cultural, Colección Conway, Papeles de Guillén de Lámport, fol. 1r.

23. We have given this document the provisional title "Proclamation of Insurrection for the Kingdom of New Spain." ITESM, fols. 40r–47v. It appears as Document 2 in this volume.

there is a temptation to believe him, given how effective his rhetoric is in turning life into theater.

During this ancien régime period in Europe, the only way to dispute rule over a kingdom was to claim sufficient title to it. And so Lamport presented himself as a brother to the king of Spain and produced various false proofs of ancestry (also found among his personal papers) very much in keeping with the role of international conspirator that he also played. The Irish soldier's contact with New Spain ignited his indignation at social injustice, summed up for him in two central themes: the oppression of the naturales and the enslaving of Africans and their descendants. He expressed his feelings in his religious poetry and wanted to move from feeling to action—as the contemporary phrase had it, "to rise with the kingdom." What we know about his insurrectional intentions stems, above all, from the "Proclamation" found among his personal papers. And, because of this stance, he is rightly considered to be a precursor of Mexican independence.

Beyond the proclamation we also have the declaration of the man who was his principal contact with the indigenous world: Ignacio Fernández Pérez, from the village of San Martín Acamistlaguacán, a blind man who worked in the mines of Taxco. Through Fernández we know that Lamport helped delegations of Indians who arrived in Mexico City to pursue some legal complaint, shaping the petitions and allegations they required. Ignacio Fernández was one of these Indians, and he and Lamport offered such services to the Taxco miners. But Fernández had another assignment from William Lamport: to organize an uprising of the Taxco miners and the Indians of San Martín:

> Don Guillén admonished this witness to arouse the naturales, or natives, of his aforementioned region, to unite three hundred or more Indian archers and assist four hundred men that he would have to seek with the utmost speed, so that with firearms and all of them gathered together they might restore this land and liberate it from the tyranny under which they labored. And the Indians should experience liberty and have all their means of support restored to them, who would [then] enjoy peace, honors and privileges, and that he should inform all of the naturales of [this possibility] and that 500 pesos should be

sought for the expenses of this war, for the benefit of them all, himself being the source from which they will secure a king of their nation named by their order and they would not pay taxes, nor other impositions on the buying or selling of products or requirements of labor because he would free them from all that.

Around August 1642 Fernández informed Lamport that everyone was enthusiastically in favor of the plan. And the miners would assemble the 500 pesos Guillén had requested through nuggets they would collect from the mines.[24]

The title on the cover that he proposed for the collection of poetry he wrote in prison, the *Regium psalterium* (which he worked on until about 1655), identifies him as "Citrae Americae Regis et Mexicanorum Imperatoris" (king of the Hithermost Americas and emperor of the Mexicans), evidence that he went on supporting his project for an uprising throughout his long imprisonment.[25]

Two parallel lines of argument, somewhat contradictory, thread through his proclamation. One is Lamport's claim to royal blood, which could make him a legitimate claimant to a throne. The other is the much more convincing argument for the democratization of the kingdom, which the revolution would secure, and squarely places him on the side of the common people.

As far as the right of the common people to usurp power, Lamport provided a philosophical-juridical justification, which the Inquisition included in its final sentence. He was denying "jurisdiction in temporal matters" to the pope because he considered invalid the papal bulls that granted dominion over "these provinces" to the kings of Spain: "It has no relevance in respect to the realm because it is neither based on a vote by the subjects nor the choice of our Lord God. It therefore follows that whoever claims to act in defense of the justice of our Lord God and of the poor, it would be just, after the tyrant is

24. "Declaration of Ignacio Fernández," AHN, no. 19, fols. 4r–8r; "Ratification of the Declaration of Ignacio Fernández," AGN, Mexico City, Inquisición, vol. 1496, fols. 52r–v.

25. "Hithermost" (Latin: Citerior) is from the name of the province of Roman Spain that lay to the east of the present-day peninsula.

censured, that the vassals should elect him who set them free as their king."[26]

Méndez Plancarte comments both on the proclamation and Lamport's poetry, and the same themes appear in both.[27] Within the code of Catholicism, they involve the special destiny of Mexico, a people in some way "chosen," and—from the viewpoint of the best and most advanced Spanish humanism—his indignation at the enslaving of Africans and their descendants and at the oppression of the Indians. The proclamation centrally contends that such oppression justifies the proposed uprising. We quote, for its relevance (with its echoes of Bartolomé de Las Casas, the apostle and defender of the Indians), his description of the condition of these naturales:

> [There are] complaints and tears from these poor naturales, caciques, and headmen, as well as republicans and commoners, who not only live deprived of their means of support, possessions, and lands but [are] miserably tyrannized and condemned to forced labor as if they were not free men but slaves themselves, who lord it over them as well, and, liable to feudal requirements and vile tributes, obligating them, by means of force and without any payment whatever for the labor of their bodies, to perpetually serve in mines, physical labor, drainage projects, plantations, sugar mills, without permitting them to become masters of that which belongs to them alone . . . at least as much as it does to us, if not more so, since the realm is theirs.[28]

With respect to the slaves, we read in Psalm 632:

> Tell me, my faithful Americans, who claim to be on the side of the Lord, why do you buy and sell men as if they were beasts?

---

26. Sentence of William Lamport, given in Riva Palacio, *Memorias de un impostor*, 338–39.

27. Méndez Plancarte, *Don Guillén de Lámport*. On Lamport's proclamation, see pages 20–23 and 100–101.

28. "Proclamation of Insurrection," ITESM, fol. 42r.

> Why do you slay in slavery men who make their confessions in
> the name of Christ? Why, against the law of God, do you
> buy Ethiopians and not wish to be bought by them?

The proclamation thus decrees that Mexican slaves will recover their
freedom:

> The same affliction and pain results from the tyrannous
> enslavement of so great a number of Negroes, mulattoes, Ber-
> bers, and other infinite [racial] branches, whose natural rights
> are usurped by the Spaniards, with little fear of God, . . . [even
> though] they are created and redeemed—and capable of the
> same glory as we are—and, as both Christians and Catholic
> members of the church, deprived of that which is more esti-
> mable than living, and that is liberty. And this forcefully calls
> on and stirs divine piety to show mercy for their serious and
> long-standing affliction and servitude . . . [and ultimately to]
> free these kingdoms and vassals from these and other infinite
> tyrannies such as now are planned and being carried out.

Lamport then, in describing his plan of action, writes,

> The fourth point: Let as many slaves as will rise in rebellion
> within these kingdoms at once be freed so as to defend and
> liberate themselves, and without excluding any condition or
> quality, whether they be African or of mixed race. Thencefor-
> ward and in conformity with their services and deeds, they will
> be as capable of receiving awards, titles of nobility, land grants,
> holy orders, lordships, and official positions on land and sea . . .
> as Spaniards themselves.

It should be noticed here that the proclamation has a certain edge
to it: it was not a description of the new society he envisioned but a
plan for achieving it. To this end the generous provisions described
were to be accompanied by ferocious warnings to those Indians,
slaves, or Spaniards who would not join the insurrection. For them
and their descendants, Lamport as king, fierce warrior that he was,
promised slavery across various generations or similar difficulties. As
for the form the new regime would take, Lamport combined a project

of liberation for the slaves, restitution of rights to the naturales, and "equality of opportunities" for all, with a system of rewards for those who would participate in the revolt, beginning with himself, who would be designated, in gratitude for his efforts, as "their prince and king."

> The twelfth point: The naturales who establish that they have been defrauded of their means of subsistence from the conquest till this very day will have their rights restored to them, and those who show themselves loyal and desirous of their liberty will be rewarded, and the caciques, nobles, and knights among them who with their own persons, their followers, and their estates would assist and further this enterprise should be rewarded with titles of marquises, dukes, counts, barons, holy orders, grandees of the kingdom, and other favors.

It is clear that the project for the new regime maintains the social hierarchies of the Spanish monarchy. The difference proposed is in the specific situation of two sectors of the population: slaves and Indians. The first would be granted freedom and the same opportunities as the rest of the population. The naturales would be considered as having been despoiled and therefore having lost means to support, preeminence, and privileges, all of which must be restored to their preconquest state. And in respect to the Spaniards, the naturales are not to be treated as an inferior sector but on a level with the Spaniards and enjoying the same rights.

Lamport's egalitarianism prefigures the declaration of José María Morelos in his "Sentimientos de la Nación" (promulgated in Chilpancingo, Mexico, on September 14, 1813): "that slavery be abolished forever, and as well the distinctions of the castes [gradations of color], leaving everyone equal, and one American will be distinguished from another American only through vice or virtue."[29]

The new regime outlined in Lamport's project would form courts where "the naturales and the freedmen will have voice and vote, just like the Spaniards," and, "as thanks for restoring their liberty and ancient rights . . . through the consent of those very naturales who are the only people as proprietaries with a vote of substance in this

29. Morelos y Pavón, "Sentimientos de la nación."

election . . . we will be elected with total fairness and untampered-with general consent, giving us possession and dominion."[30]

In Lamport's plan the hierarchies would be neither firmly fixed nor exclusive categories but linked to "equality of opportunities" and an epic ideal: all men are free and the "offspring of their own exploits":

> The thirteenth point: The same with the other classes of people, of whatever quality or condition they may be, without there being for anyone in the future any inequality in the matter of being capable of merited reward, as we have said, for all men are free from now on and the offspring of their own exploits and as capable as the Spaniards of ecclesiastical as well as secular and military achievement.

It was impossible for this surprising precursor of Latin American independence and champion of social justice (before the term took on its modern meaning) to generate a program so radical and comprehensive in a vacuum. We can trace the course of his gradual radicalization across the short space of his two years of freedom (1640–42) before his arrest. In his letters to the king, we find passages such as the following: "Enough, oh sovereign lord, with such and so royal clemency toward the sterile transgressors of your sublime laws! Unleash, lord, the lightning bolt of your powerful arm and make up for so many losses with punishments. . . . Punish ministers so voracious and greedy that they barbarously swallow the very strength of your kingdoms that are so fecund, depriving Your Sublime Majesty and your oppressed vassals of the rights and justice that you hold and administer, while they violate positive privileges human and divine."[31]

In other writings he accuses the ministers of making a business out of reselling various products, while the populace subsisted in misery: "There is now no vassal or Indian who has enough to support himself." He would concentrate on denouncing the excessive taxes on cacao and the positions held by people with no capacity to fill them, such as the judge of the mulattoes and mestizos, the official in charge

30. "Proclamation of Insurrection," ITESM, fol. 41r.
31. Drafts of letters to the king of Spain, ITESM, fols. 156r, 156v.

of the royal monopoly on playing cards, "the official [who oversees
the production and sale] of pulque who is [merely] the viceroy's
stable boy," while there are "poor people who can lay claim to the
highest merits courting those cold tiles of the palace and sighing to
heaven."[32]

We have already considered the substantial education, suffused
with reformist idealism, of Lamport at various European schools. A
recent biographer of Juan de Palafox, Cayetana Álvarez de Toledo,
writes that the political agitation in New Spain during those years
was kindled by the publication of a work by Palafox, in which he
risks making a bold criticism of authority, apparently directed against
the Count-Duke of Olivares. The book was *Historia real sagrada: Luz
de principes y subditos* (Sacred royal history: Light for princes and
subjects), which was published in Puebla in 1643. In this *Historia real
sagrada*, the bishop developed his notion of a kingdom with defined
and agreed-on limits. If they did in fact know each other, it is possible
that Lamport and Palafox discussed the ideas contained in the bishop's recently completed book.

With Lamport in prison, Palafox in 1647 sent a denunciation to
Madrid against those trying to bring accusations against him personally, including most of the inquisitors also persecuting Lamport. He
argued against the claims of these men for widening their authority
over society through their abusive interpretation of what were considered "articles of faith." His argumentation is an excellent defense
of that open space for reflection and political criticism that the
inquisitors wanted to cut off: "It thus being permitted and licit, if it is
done with due moderation and prudence, to dispute the power of the
tribunals and purpose competing jurisdictions and, what is more, the
power of the supreme heads [of society] such as pontiffs and kings,
and so there are entire treatises on the subject [disputing their power
and jurisdiction] in [the corpus of] the law. And between reasonable
people one can discuss and dispute in that prudent, Christian, and
considerate mode."[33]

To these ideas in defense of individual reflection and debate, we
must add the separation of realms already discussed—the temporary

32. Ibid., fols. 156r–v, 161. Pulque is a traditional Mexican alcoholic beverage,
made by fermenting the sap of the maguey cactus.
33. Medina, *Historia del Tribunal*, 245–46.

breakaway of Portugal and Catalonia—and the thinking of Las Casas, Francisco de Vitoria, and the other Spanish humanists of a century before (though we do not know whether Lamport was acquainted with them) and above all the violent Irish Rebellion that began in 1641. In these ideas and events we can look for the roots of his bold imagination.

Lamport planned his escape and implemented it on "the night of the first day of Christmas," 1650. He took various sheets of paper with him, which, during the previous three months, he had filled as best as he could, writing in miniscule handwriting and using every inch of space. (As incredible as it may seem, these invaluable documents can still be consulted in archives.) They contain a formally elaborated juridical complaint, repeated various times, against the inquisitors of the tribunal of the Holy Inquisition of Mexico and against their useless inspector, the archbishop Juan de Mañozca, who died around the same time.[34]

William Lamport escaped to circulate his denunciation and perhaps achieve his major objective: the imprisonment of the inquisitors, the return of confiscated possessions (now in the private hands of the inquisitors) to the accused Portuguese crypto-Jews as well as their liberation, and also of course his own liberty. It was another attempt at a small revolution, a master stroke meant to unleash a profound change in the structures of power within New Spain.

After eight years in captivity, the escaped "criminal," having fled with his cellmate, Diego Pinto, got as far as the bedroom of the viceroy.[35] According to Pinto's declaration,

> And they had gone together (he does not remember whether it was by Relox Street or Santo Domingo Street) to the palace at three in the morning and that Don Guillén had mounted to the room of the lord viceroy and told the soldier of the guard

34. The judicial complaint, titled by Lamport as "Pregón de los justos jucios de Dios que castigue a quien lo quitare" (Proclamation of the Just Judgments of God: May He Punish Whoever Would Tear It Down) can be found in AGN, vol. 1497, file 1, fol. 8r. There is a copy in AHN, no. 24, fols. 7r–8v. The translation is Document 3 in this volume. The other petitions, which were transcribed immediately afterward, can be found in AHN, no. 24, fols. 8v–13r, 13r–20v.

35. Diego Pinto was the husband of the lay sister María Romero. Diego, María, and her sister Josefa all died in prison. Rubial García, *Profetisas y solitarios.*

that he came from Veracruz with a document from Havana for His Excellency that was of great import in the service of God and king and that it must be delivered that instant. And when the soldier of the guard told him that the viceroy had just been gambling and was now resting, the aforesaid Don Guillén had said that nevertheless he should call and advise him [that he had arrived], as the soldier of the guard then did.[36]

They affixed other pages to the door of the Metropolitan Cathedral and on a corner of Tacuba Street and other places "in the usual streets," said a master tailor who testified against him: "He arrived at the great church and placed his petition on the door in front of the stone cross, without saying what substance he had used to attach it. And when he had reached said stone cross, he had asked the aforementioned Diego Pinto what cross this was? Which he had neither seen nor knew of before. And the response was that it was the cross that had been placed there by the lord archbishop. And the aforesaid Don Guillén responded, although a thief set you here, I worship you."[37]

We have an unusually detailed account of Lamport's few hours of freedom. He wore several changes of clothing, one on top of the other, some of it brand new, which aroused considerable suspicion among his inquisitors. (It was later clarified that he had been buying clothes with the remains of his living allowance.) He was drenched, covered in mud, and wounded in one hand. He had immediately changed his clothes after entering the humble dwelling of some acquaintances. The whole neighborhood of Santa María la Redonda knew about the apparition of this "Jew," who was carrying a huge bundle of bedsheets (perhaps used for his getaway) and clothing. Among those providing information about his arrival and appearance were an Indian midwife and an Indian headman in the neighborhood who had held the office of neighborhood judge.

Lamport dined, slept, had his breakfast, and tried to follow his plan of setting out for San Antonio in Veracruz. Francisco de Garnica, the traitorous tailor, told Lamport that he did not know where that place might be. "And he said to him, have you not heard about where the

---

36. "Declaration of Francisco de Garnica," AHN, no. 24, fol. 35r.
37. Ibid., fols. 32v, 35v.

Negroes live near Veracruz, whose captain is a mulatto named Diego de Jal (he does not remember the surname that he gave him). And this witness said that he did not know but that Guillén was right, that the said mulatto was the son of a negro named Ñanga, who was hanged in this city because he was a fugitive slave (*cimarrón*) who had risen with other slaves in rebellion."[38]

Diego de Jal must have been a successor to Yanga (or Ñanga), a Congolese prince who had founded the village of fugitive slaves (with the agreement of the viceroy Don Luis de Velasco) called San Lorenzo de los Negros (today Yanga in the state of Veracruz). Its establishment was officially legitimized by the viceroy Marquis of Cerralvo in 1630. The stated San Antonio location could have been a place nearby.

The Inquisition immediately circulated the most severe threats against anyone who might hide Lamport, and he fell into their hands in a matter of hours: "They searched his pouch and found some pieces of eight and some single papers hidden at his chest between his jacket and his doublet and folded into four parts."[39] In the report of the Inquisition about this "bundle of papers," which was examined "very minutely," we read that "in all the said papers nothing was found relating to his case, nor to the Holy Office nor to his ministers, because they were all Latin verses, hymns in Latin, verses in Castilian with different intentions and in praise of the most holy Virgin."[40]

This handful of verses in Latin and Spanish seized by the tribunal of the Inquisition in 1650 seems to have been lost. But between 1652 and 1655 Lamport produced 918 more Latin psalms, composed in prison and hidden from his jailors, forming a book he named *Regium psalterium* (Royal psalter). Since they would no longer give him any paper, he wrote them on bedsheets "of white linen," says the dossier of the Inquisition. Luis González Obregón, in his *Don Guillén de Lámport*, notes that the bedsheets were lost, but the tribunal of the Inquisition made a copy of 117 pages, which they added to the second volume of his case file.[41]

---

38. Ibid., fol. 38r.
39. Pieces of eight are silver coins worth eight Spanish reales.
40. "Declaration of Hernando de la Fuente," warden of the secret jails, AHN, no. 24, fol. 42v.
41. *Regium psalterium*, AGN, vol. 1497, file 1, fols. 371r–489v. In a margin of his copy of *D. Guillén de Lámport*, by González Obregón, Lord Conway wrote in

Rodrigo Ruíz de Zepeda Martínez, who wrote the Inquisition report after Lamport's execution, could not help admiring the manner in which he managed to continue writing in prison. In reference to the petitions that Lamport affixed to doors during his brief spell of freedom in 1650 and also to his writing of the 918 Latin psalms, Ruíz de Zepeda wrote that Lamport used glued-together smoking paper as writing sheets; made ink out of soot, honey, and water; and used sharpened chicken feathers as pens "with such good results that he was able to write all these works very intelligibly."[42]

A Tireless Defender of His Fellow Prisoners

From William Lamport's papers a complete and detailed history emerges—lucid, courageous, and compassionate—of the systematic destruction of the Portuguese crypto-Jewish community of Mexico in the years 1642–49. In the *gran auto-da-fé* of 1649, a total of 109 prisoners were condemned to different sentences. As already stated, at least 10 died in prison in the meantime—confirming Lamport's denunciation of the dreadful jail conditions and the tortures—so, if the prisoners were condemned to die, then either their bones or their effigy was humiliated and burned in the pyre. Of the convicted, 13 people were actually executed.[43] Lamport had intimate knowledge of the campaign against the crypto-Jewish financiers, and it was his misfortune to share their eventual fate. Of the imprisonment of Francisco Nieto, an eighty-year-old man, he writes,

> They tortured him, with the expectation that they could force so elderly a man to prevaricate and give them, through false testimony, some case against others whom they wanted to ensnare. But they found themselves frustrated. They broke his

reference to the *Regium psalterium*: "Stolen from the AGN." If so, was it recovered by Lord Conway? It was he, after all, who showed the *Regium psalterium* to Méndez Plancarte, on the basis of which he published his selection and study. A complete copy of the *Regium psalterium* can be found in AHN, no. 26, fols. 179r–356r.

42. Ruíz de Zepeda Martínez, *Auto general de la fee*, 57v.

43. All the quotations in this section are taken from "Criminal Complaint," AHN. See also "Prison Communications," AGN, vol. 1496, fols. 120r–247v. García-Molina Riquelme, *Hogueras de la Inquisición*, provides additional information.

arm . . . and after he had been tortured and broken to pieces, the treacherous murderers put him alone in a cell, with no one to give him any human assistance. It was two and a half years before he could use his hands and . . . he had to lower his face into his plate [to eat]. And when he tried to drink, he would spill the water in bed on himself, and when getting up to relieve himself he would fall and suffer many head wounds and broke his already injured hand, and they would find him laid out nude in the middle of his cell, without the strength to return to his bed.[44]

His human sympathy and his proximity, as a direct witness, to the rounding up of the Portuguese crypto-Jews gave Lamport a clear perspective on this sad tangle of denunciations to which the prisoners were driven by fear and the total absence of any personal rights. Lamport provides a long and minutely detailed report, including the names of the numerous accused and their torturers and the quantities of money and goods seized from them in each case: an accurate, formal, and detailed denunciation all the more remarkable because of the conditions under which it was written. One example: "They circumcised Francisco de León during a torture session and offered as a [justifiable] cause that he looked at the sky while before the tribunal, the action of a Jew [they declared], and the witness was [the inquisitor] Mañozca." He writes fervently of inquisitors' rapaciousness:

Oh holy men of Holy Office! With wealthy men whom they arrested inland, they sacked their stores by night, and the holy ministers, by day, distributed the treasures among their lady friends. And when someone appearing before the holy tribunal spoke of the robbery committed against his store, to the tune of more than 100,000 pesos, of how they carried away bundles and sacks by night, they responded, "This is the way it is done." . . . The sheriff and his secretary registered the boxes behind closed doors and, to the holy tribunal, vouched for the carriages laden with rich treasure, extending even to trousers adorned with crimson decorations, gold, silver, and jewels.

44. "Criminal Complaint," AHN, no. 24, fols. 92v–93r.

After giving a long list, painful to read, of the victims' names, Lamport continues with stories of the prisoners, "whose tragedies, each one more pitiful than the last in conveying pain, grief, horror, and pity to this and future centuries. With privation and neglect and torture and starvation and tyrannous behavior, they killed the hermit Fernando de Goiz; Isabel Nuñez, the wife of Luis Pers; Doña Catalina; Doña Blanca de la Veracruz and María la Blanca, whom her mother drowned in the prison because no one prevented it; Diego Córrez; Gonzalo Váez. Doña Ana, the deaf woman, who was the mother of the Blanca woman, they drove to madness . . . and Doña Ana died insane."[45]

And a description follows of more sufferings: "And those who did not die at once remained without hope, those injured by tortures, almost a hundred people; they left them uncared for for three days so that they became victims of cancer, and about many of them the Holy Office circulated the rumor that they had died of plague, whereas hunger was the true cause." The description day by day, compassionate and detailed, includes an account of food denied to the sick, the rotten eggs that they made them pay for double the price of fresh ones, the chickens they allowed "that had drowned in the sewers." "And often they gave them as drink pestilential and rotten water in which they had washed other things so that their entrails might rot . . . and so atrocious was their greed that they did not wrap those who died in a sheet of their own linen but in a mat, and then they threw them into a hidden pit for disposal."[46]

Lamport's accounts of how the victims were robbed of their possessions and the conditions of their imprisonment also include numerous reconstructed dialogues, some of them even grimly humorous, with a sense of drama. For example, he tells the story of the arrest of a mulatto tobacco vendor, Gerónimo Álvarez, a Portuguese who knew no Spanish, and he reconstructs the dialogues, in Portuguese, between the inquisitors and this man who could not understand a word they said and who had been informed of various arrests by a "Chinese woman" and came voluntarily to the chambers of the Inquisition to buy his freedom ("so that you do not do me any harm, I would give you 200 pesos"). And then before anything else

45. Ibid., fols. 268r, 266r, 269r.
46. Ibid., fols. 269r–269v.

he was circumcised by "two guardian angels who circumcise as many blessed men as they want, the surgeon Castillo and Juan Correa, a mulatto barber." The unfortunate tobacco vendor unleashed curses against the Chinese woman: "She was unfaithful to me, and I gave her some money every day." Lamport describes the following scene:

> And with the unfortunate man not understanding either the word "Jew" or the word "circumcised" . . . they said to him then, "You are a Jew. Perform Jewish ceremonies." To which he answered, "You say I am a Jew?" And they responded, "Yes." And it should be noted that in the southern ocean sailed by the aforesaid mulatto, there is a fish they call the Portuguese. It swims at the surface of the water, and it feeds on flies. [The word "Portuguese," as a result of the persecutions by the Inquisition, was then popularly identified with the word "Jew."] The aforementioned mulatto then stretched out on the ground and, opening his mouth as if he were demonstrating how to catch flies and moving his body as if he were swimming, he said, "These are the ceremonies of the Jews."

This is how Lamport depicts his own captivity: "And there is no language that can describe the horrors committed against me, and it was nothing compared to [what was practiced on] the others, always in dank cells, great numbers of Caribbean rats gnawing at my feet; twice they tried to poison me; they held back my allowance (amounting to half a real's worth) over a period of four months; they took away my clothing allowance. . . . The suffering from solitude exceeded everything under the sun, for through this means alone they made many deny their faith and elicited false testimony from them."[47]

In great detail and in a sarcastic tone, he describes the various stages of his imprisonment. The inquisitors who destroyed his life were named Domingo Vélez de Assas y Argos, Juan Sáenz de Mañozca, Francisco de Estrada y Escobedo, and Eugenio de Sarabia. When they brought him for the first time before the tribunal, they did not let him speak: "And they remained silent, as representatives of severe divinity." The inquisitors were not exempt from his invectives or from his educated and acute mind—nor from his desperation

47. Ibid., fols. 105r–v, 19r–v.

or from a measure of suicidal theatricality: "On presenting me [before the tribunal], they uttered a great prologue, saying that I should neither speak nor call out to God. And then I uttered a smiling and furious shriek."[48]

They were dealing with a learned man, a scholar who knew more about theology than they did. In commenting on the sins and crimes of the inquisitors, Lamport quotes Saint Augustine, Saint Gregory, Nicholas of Lyra, Seneca, and the books of the holy scriptures, supplying extract references, as well as Saint Luke, Saint Matthew, the psalms, Saint Jerome, Saint Thomas, Plato, Saint Athanasius, Saint Paul, Boethius, Tertullian, Saint Cyprian, and Albertus Magnus. Moreover, Lamport unravels the logic of the inquisitors: they could not confiscate goods of anyone who proved themselves to be Catholics, hence the inquisitors forcing confessions of Judaism from their prisoners. The secret law of the Inquisition guaranteed total impunity to the inquisitors. No one was exempt. "If they are discovered: death and whippings; if they dispute [the charges]: death and whippings; if they resist the frauds and heresies [of the inquisitors] and are not willing to become apostates: shackles, chains, hunger, nudity, tortures, and burning at the stake."[49]

But Lamport's denunciation is also deeper and more noble. He goes into what these forced confessions mean, in philosophical, moral, and juridical terms. In the first place, he says, "It is an abominable heresy that, in order to conceal their deceit, they dare to probe the depths of the heart reserved for [the scrutiny] of God, as if the response to these questions were not violating and damning their atrocious souls even more."[50] Contained in this statement are various ideas now considered modern: that a confession obtained by torture is not valid but also that no one has the right to probe "the depths of the heart reserved for [the scrutiny] of God"—that is to say that each person has the right to retain and protect their own secrets. And, further, every person is innocent unless proven guilty with legitimate motives and methods.

He goes deeper, because the fundamental theme in the jail where he stayed was obviously the issue of "the Jew." Lamport offers a

48. Ibid., fols. 48r–v.
49. Ibid., fol. 106r.
50. Ibid., fols. 95v–96r.

number of rhetorical turns on the subject. One thing that he cannot do, in the middle of the seventeenth century and in a realm subject to the Spanish Crown, is defend the right of Jews to continue being Jews. But at the end of his intricate argument, it appears that the matter of whether or not one is or is not a Jew is a minor one, because in any case Christians are not themselves behaving like Christians: "Because there in that sacred and secret house, there is nothing that smacks of a Christian; no one enters to preach or argue with anyone, and there is no reason to do so, because [these Jews] are better Catholics than many men of faith."[51]

For Lamport, to be a Catholic in the first place means conducting oneself in the correct manner, and therefore the first who ought to be considered as lacking in faith are the inquisitors themselves. He also discusses the "Judaizing" practices emphasized by the inquisitors. The first of them is fasting, which they attribute to Jews. Here he displays a profound knowledge of the ethnic roots of Christianity, in weaving his arguments on the question of *not being a Jew*: fasting, he asserts, is Christian; it has nothing to do with Judaism. Nor, he claims, does circumcision! He quotes a history of Ethiopia "by the very learned Urrieta, a Dominican," which ascribes the legendary name of Prester John to the emperor of Ethiopia—Lamport must be quoting from memory when he says,

> They are no more Jews than the Negroes of Ethiopia in the realm of Prester John, who are the purest Christians and most faithful to the church and fast every day as do the Jews, and the Moors also fast and circumcise themselves when they are baptized. And the aforesaid Catholic emperor [Prester John] sent Zagazabo, the Black bishop and Catholic prelate of Ethiopia, to the holy Roman apostolic seat in order, yet again, to offer his obedience . . . and established a college in Rome that they name in their native language, and they perform mass very differently from the Greek and the Latin [traditions]. And His Holiness that bishop made his protestation of the faith in a manner practiced among Catholics since the time of Saint Thomas, who himself preached to and converted the eunuch of

Queen Candace, daughter of the Black king who was guided by the star to the manger of our Lord.[52]

Lamport recounts the questions and answers between His Holiness and Bishop Zagazabo concerning fasting and circumcision ("and he answered that it was because our Lord Jesus Christ was circumcised and baptized, and even women were circumcised because they have, he says, in the genital area a glandular and fleshy part suitable for circumcision").[53] Jesus Christ then was circumcised and baptized; one might say he was equally Jewish and Catholic. If that could be the case with him, why not with others? The underlying argument in Lamport's exposition is that Christianity is really an act of faith, and both Black Ethiopians and the ancient Jews could belong to its generously receptive body of belief—or else that being Jewish is an ancient ethnic variant within the conjunction of peoples, practices, and beliefs that constituted Christianity.

Lamport also offers the case of Juan de León, "Jew by nationality, but a citizen of Pisa." Woven into the dramatic account of his arrest and condemnation, he argues that this man neither relapsed nor disguised himself, but that here was a case of a Jew who wanted to convert. Another of his arguments was that being a Jew involved a series of practices that the prisoners could not perform, and therefore they could not be considered Jews, just as "one cannot be a Christian without baptism."[54]

He recalls the converted Jews wandering the length of Europe in trying to flee various persecutions and remembers an event during his years as a soldier in the service of the cardinal infante Don Ferdinando de Austria, the brother of King Philip IV ("living examples that I transmit to the world as one who has seen and traveled around foreign realms"):

> When the lord infante traveled through Flanders across the realms and provinces of the Grisons, who are all heretics, an infinite number of Portuguese came out to meet him, the most powerful men who supported these realms, and, understanding

52. Ibid., fols. 97r, 97v.
53. Ibid., fol. 97v.
54. Ibid., fols. 100v–102r.

the natural obeisance [owed] to the king and therefore to his brother, they offered His Holiness hospitality in their houses. And when he asked them why they had deserted their king, they answered that through the abominations and rapacity of the Inquisition, under the cover of secrecy, [based on] some little pieces of paper or none at all and through [the inquisitors'] false inductions, they were liable every day to being disgraced or having their lives and properties taken from them and having to leave their children at [someone's] door, and for this reason they were treated with violence far from their fatherland, king and people of their own blood. And then they brought His Holiness to their chapels, with their rich and costly adornment that each one had, together with its chaplain, and where they heard mass, and they told him they were living in a land where they could live as they wished, and that if they were Jews as those of the Holy Secret [Inquisition] tried [to assert], they would not live as Catholics since they were able to live [here] with freedom of conscience. And they offered His Highness two million in gold, if he needed that money on his way to Flanders, and the generous prince, having accepted the gift, was moved as a witness to it all. And he said, "My brother, may God protect him, is bewitched and Spain is blind."[55]

In such writings we can discern the ideas of this man, endowed with a substantial education and knowledge of Ireland, England, Spain, France, Belgium, Venice, Germany, Switzerland, and the Low Countries, who would surely be pained to remember those parts of the world where one could, as he himself says, "live with freedom of conscience." His unprecedented, insistent, and multifaceted defense of the Jews is not surprising in an Irish Catholic voluntarily taking refuge under the protection of King Philip IV, whose court cultivated arts and letters. With experience of a number of peoples who formed the vast kingdoms of this monarchy that was in the process of collapsing and dismembering, Lamport, in good faith, was seeking the adoption of more inclusive policies. And he probably saw a similarity between these exiled Jews, who were fleeing persecution and had no

55. Ibid., fols. 104r–v. The Grisons are nowadays a canton in Switzerland.

nation and took refuge in the mercy of the Spanish monarchy, and the Irish Catholics, voluntary vassals of Philip III and Philip IV.

History Has Not Done Him Justice

William Lamport was an Irish warrior of ancient lineage, outstanding student and adventurer, fierce soldier in the service of the king of Spain, theologian, poet, international political agent or conspirator, revolutionary in two realms—a man who denounced the Holy Inquisition from within its own dungeons and during its most aggressive period. Nevertheless, his life and works were little remarked on until the very close of the twentieth century. Most of his deeds were repeatedly denied by the Inquisition, in the hundreds of pages of his trial, and his posthumous reputation was ruined. Upon reading him boasting of his exploits, my tendency, as would be the case for most historians, was to consider him to be lying or at least strongly exaggerating. Only after considering the logic of his claims in their historical context did I start to believe he was mostly telling the truth. And so it was that, for most of Mexican history, the imputations of Lamport's discreditors have stayed with him. He has been called a madman, a fantasist, a mythomaniac.

This unjust reputation was established in modern times by the Mexican Vicente Riva Palacio (1832–96). This historian (and soldier) studied the volumes on Lamport's trial. He wrote a novel of romantic interludes that accepts the coarsest accusations of the Inquisition as absolute and admirable truths. His title alone proves our point: *Memorias de un impostor, Don Guillén de Lámport, rey de México* (Memoirs of an impostor, Don Guillén de Lámport, king of Mexico). The Riva Palacio novel resurrected the memory of Lamport and interested the long-standing Mexican president Porfirio Díaz, when planning the commemoration of the first centennial of Mexican Independence in 1910. Along with the nationalist sculptures intended to accompany the famous monuments of the Angel of Independence in Mexico City, he decided to add a representation of Lamport on the pyre of the Inquisition, with a statue seven feet high. The sculpture was made, but Lamport wasn't in the end accepted as ranking among the great heroes of independence. A decision was then taken to set the statue by itself within the chamber at the base of the column of the angel, among the mortal remains of many of those same heroes. Ironically, his statue was thus hidden within the heart of the main symbol of Mexican independence. In 2010, the year of the bicentennial, there was discussion about moving the statue from that location, but this came to nothing. A theater piece was performed that year, called *Lámport o de cómo colarse a la historia* (Lamport, or how to gate-crash history).

After Riva Palacio, Luis González Obregón (1865–1938) and the Chilean José Toribio Medina (1852–1930) were his best biographers. González Obregón rectified his biography, clearing it of the extravagant baggage added by Riva Palacio, and Medina presented him correctly as a rebel advocating independence. In the middle of the twentieth century, Gabriel Méndez Plancarte produced a carefully edited transcription and translation of a selection of Lamport's Latin poetry and commented on his "Proclamation." Then came half a century of silence, until in 1999 the Italian Fabio Troncarelli wrote a thorough and excellently documented book on Lamport. His book triggered a Lamport revival, in part of which my own work should be counted, of studies of his life and the curation and publication of the writings. Also worthy of mention are the publications by Gerard Ronan, Sarah Cline, Vázquez Guillén, Ryan Dominic Crewe, and Olivia Isidro Vázquez. Finally, Gonzalo Lizardo has given us an excellent edition of Lamport's masterwork, *Cristiano desagravio y retractaciones* (Christian atonement and retractions), and in 2020 a beautiful novel on the life and writings of Lamport. It is time to give William Lamport his proper place in history as an outstanding humanist fighter and as a fine author. With the publication and translation of some of his most exemplary writings, we are trying to contribute to this restitution.

On This Edition

At the time of his death at the hands of the Holy Inquisition, William Lamport left most of his writings behind in Mexico: political, literary, and personal. Moreover, his many appearances before the tribunal of the Holy Inquisition were faithfully transcribed and are extensive documents of great value.

Despite his exceptional life and unquestionable literary skill, Lamport's works have not been thoroughly explored and published. To this date the only publications are Méndez Plancarte's anthology of his prison poetry and the proclamation for the independence of

New Spain, along with a general study on the man and his writings, published in 1948; my own Spanish-language book, published in 2012, which includes four writings by Lamport; and Lizardo's annotated transcription and edition of the *Cristiano desagravio*.[56]

The writings Lamport composed in Mexico can be found in two collections: the Instituto Tecnológico y de Estudios Superiores de Monterrey (ITESM), an important university in Monterrey, Nuevo León, Mexico; and the Archivo General de la Nación (AGN) in Mexico City. A summary of both collections follows.

Papeles de Guillén de Lámport, Colección Conway, Biblioteca Cervantina, Patrimonio Cultural, ITESM

Lamport arrived in Mexico in 1640. Until 1642 (when he was imprisoned on Sunday, October 26), we can document his life primarily through his personal papers discovered in a wood chest, the contents of which were included in the records of his trial. Among these papers can be found something of the splendors of his European adventures but also a humble search for employment. There is a short book on military tactics composed by Lamport, meant to help him obtain a military appointment, a homemade rendering of his family's heraldic shield, and the formal documentation of his personal qualities and achievements, probably all designed to aid him in his quest for employment. Two documents in this collection stand out, which we publish in this edition for the first time complete, translated into English from the original Spanish.

Gilbert Nugent, representative of the Irish nobles at the court of King Philip IV, presented a petition toward the end of 1639, requesting the king's military support for the planned uprising against the English occupation. Documentation in Spain and elsewhere confirms the existence of the petition, but, as far as we know, the original has not been found in the European archives, save for a few extracts included in the contemporary commentaries on the petition. We found the petition among those Mexican papers.[57] The trunk also contained the proclamation of independence for New Spain that so

---

56. Méndez Plancarte, *Don Guillén de Lámport*; Martínez Baracs, *Don Guillén de Lamport*; Lombardo, *Cristiano desagravio*.

57. There have been various publications on these events, particularly Mesa Gallego, *Spanish Armies*; Pérez Tostado, *Irish Influence*; Troncarelli and Pérez Tostado, "Plot Without Capriccio."

alarmed the authorities. It is only one among these documents on the subject; without more context one could almost mistake it for a divertimento. But its true insurrectional intention is confirmed by the testimony of various witnesses at his trial.

The Holy Inquisition had the papers from the trunk sewn together to preserve their unity and added to the prosecutor's documentation for Lamport's appearance before the court. This collection was later removed from storage and put up for sale. It ended up in private hands, ultimately in those of Lord Conway, an oil magnate with a strong interest in history, who donated them (along with his own personal library and other valuable writings) to the Biblioteca Cervantina of the ITESM.

Inquisición, Archivo General de la Nación

Lamport was imprisoned from 1642 to 1659, when he was burned at the stake by order of the tribunal of the Holy Inquisition. The AGN preserves the bulky file, to be found mainly in two large collections, volumes 1496 and 1497 of the annals of the Inquisition.

The file contains the minutiae of his lengthy trial: accusations, testimonies, declarations by the defendant, and confiscated documents. Lamport used the hearings to denounce the inquisitors and present a defense of himself and all others thrown into the Inquisition prisons. Lamport's arrest coincided with a wave of persecution against "secret Jews" (*marranos*), for their presumed (and banned) practice of Judaism, which culminated in the great auto-da-fé of April 1649, the largest of such mass executions by burning in the history of New Spain. Lamport's statements, in defense of himself and the other prisoners, are of great humanitarian, theological, and spiritual value.

Among the AGN files are the original writings prepared in various copies by Lamport, to be put up in different public places, as his judicial defense for his escape in December 1650. We publish here an English translation of the best-preserved version, titled by Lamport "Proclamation of the Just Judgments of God: May He Punish Whoever Would Tear It Down."

Lamport's major poetry corpus, in Latin, is certainly his *Regium psalterium*, originally written on bedsheets during his incarceration. The Holy Office had the whole piece carefully transcribed and preserved among the files of the trial. We here publish the title page and twenty of its 918 psalms and hymns, translated from Latin into

English. In Hank Heifetz's new translations, the originality and nuances of Lamport's poetry are powerfully presented.

Another substantial addition to this English-language edition is the translation of what is perhaps Lamport's most important poem in Spanish. It is untitled but we are adopting its first line as its title: *Alcides magno, y del olimpo puro*, or *Great Alcides, and the Pure Olympian*. It introduces Lamport's major literary work in prose, also composed in prison: the *Cristiano desagravio y retractaciones*, a consummate work of great literary ambition and a subtle and devastating satire against his executioners, the inquisitors of New Spain.[58] Finally, we publish an excerpt from the book issued after his execution by Rodrigo Ruíz de Zepeda Martínez, assigned by the Holy Office as the defense of Lamport during the trial.

A Note on Lamport's Name
To various declarations before the tribunal of the Holy Inquisition, William Lamport signed his name as Don Guillén Lombardo de Guzmán and, on the notices he posted during his one day of freedom, Don Guillén Lombardo. But these are adaptations into Spanish of his Irish name, William Lamport. His principal Mexican biographers, Luis González Obregón and Vicente Riva Palacio, called him Guillén de Lámport. (In the Spanish edition of the present book I also adopted the name Guillén de Lámport.) I have used his Irish name in this edition except where an issue of correct identification or ascription requires a Hispanicized form.

---

58. The Biblioteca Digital Mexicana (bdmx.mx) has a facsimile online of the complete *Cristiano desagravio*, along with its transcription by Gonzalo Lizardo, who published his annotated edition in 2017.

William Lamport was the son and grandson of Irish revolutionaries and himself one of the Wild Geese. The English conquest of Ireland, the proscription of Catholicism, the confiscation of the estates, and the closing of institutions of Irish Catholics created this Irish diaspora. Many of them, soldiers as they were, entered as mercenaries into the service of the king of Spain, the foremost Catholic monarch of the time. Charles I of England condemned Lamport to death when he was a student in London for writings refuting the legitimacy of the English invasion of Ireland. He had to flee the country and continue his studies in Spain. He came to be accepted at the university attended by nobles of the Spanish court, during which time he developed a friendship with the Count-Duke of Olivares, the king's favorite. And Lamport participated with distinction in the Irish contingent of the Royal Army in the Eighty Years' War.

Between 1639 and 1640 an emissary of the Irish Catholic nobility (one of the "titles [of nobility]" mentioned in the document), Gilberto Nugencio, or Gilbert Nugent, went to Madrid with the intention of persuading the Count-Duke of Olivares to secure royal support for the coming Irish uprising. Lamport also figured in this delicate attempt at persuasion.

The text, written in Spanish in the tightly condensed handwriting Lamport used in his personal papers, is a copy of the proposal or memorial delivered to the count-duke or the king himself, very likely written by Gilbert Nugent, perhaps with Lamport's help. Although it is known to specialists, my Spanish-language monograph and this

FIG. 2 First page of the "Proposal to King Philip IV for the Liberation of Ireland." ITESM, fol. 153r.

English-language edition would seem to be the first publication of the text in its entirety.

The Irish uprising began on October 23, 1641. It was very bloody and came close to succeeding but was put down between 1649 and 1653 by the invading army of Oliver Cromwell. Throughout the rest of the century, Irish soldiers flocked to the service of Spain. Also among Lamport's private papers is an authorization directed to Nugent from the nobles of Ireland, allowing him to negotiate support from the Spanish Crown for the uprising. Lamport very likely wrote this authorization. It is a preliminary draft in Spanish and English, dated July 4, 1639.[1]

My Lord,

The person known to Your Majesty presents, in the name of the gentlemen and Catholics of the realm of Ireland, the miserable and painful condition that they endure, which obliges them not to vengeance or infamous treason but to a licit enterprise meant to expand and defend the holy Catholic faith, in order to evade the captivity and tyranny they suffer, to see themselves free of such abominable servitude, to forestall new humiliations that [their tormenters] invent, [and] to avenge the injuries committed against heaven itself.[2]

So that they may not see their sons raised and instructed in the law of heretics, the fathers of families pay a silver *real* every Sunday so that each member of their household may hear mass. Catholic burials, weddings, and baptisms are forbidden; priests are expelled; the sacraments are destroyed; and the Irishman is deprived of every religious consolation. If they do not attend the temples of the heretics, they persecute them with insults, expel them from the land, and after that they ruin them.

If one is poor, they condemn him to labor until he is ransomed with his blood. All their efforts in parliament are bent on trying to stamp papists out of that realm. If the nobility opposes, it is accused of disloyalty to the king. Its entire government and [the weight of] its hand is tyranny. Dealings with the Irish by sea or land are prohibited, any contact with other nations impeded.

1. "Proposal to King Philip IV for the Liberation of Ireland," ITESM, fol. 160r.
2. Ibid., fols. 153r–154v. The original document is untitled. The paleography is by Andrea Martínez Baracs.

With new plantations they usurp the lands of the former knights, and he who was yesterday a gentleman now finds himself a miserable slave. If the noble [Irishman] argues with them because of their insolent actions, then he is a traitor and in contact with Spain, and they strip him of his life. If [the Irish] say that they are being tyrannized, they speak "treason" and [the Irish] die. For two *reales* they hang an accused Irishman. Everything, to put down the Irish nation!

If an ounce of powder, a bullet, or any arms are found in their possession, then they die without any human recourse. Those who are innocent and convicted and who die in that place every year could compose a numerous army. No special privilege or any law protects them. The products of the realm have to pass through the hands of the English. The Dutch and other nations have free access to the fishing grounds, which is denied to the original inhabitants. The mines, which are very rich and of every sort, are managed by the English for their own profit, making use of the Irish Catholics as slaves until they die at their labors. And [though it is] the most fertile and powerful kingdom in the world, they proclaim it to be poor and infertile, in order to undermine [the Irish] prizing of it and so that this prizing not assist [the Irish] in dispossessing the tyrannical possessors.

A thousand titled nobles inhabit this realm with their powerful estates, a number that exceeds the titled nobles of England, Wales, and Scotland together. And with all this power, they are tyrannized because they lack a military leader who can encourage their valor and their [desire for] liberty. The virgins themselves are violated (an excess to which the most barbarous cruelty of the heathen never reached in their persecution of the church) for resisting the fury of the heretics. And all bewail a lust so common and inhuman.

These and other infinite affronts and extortions that do not [. . .] so as not to weary Your Majesty, they have reduced the nobility and the realm to such extreme paroxysms [. . .] in the matter of a remedy, they despair of it unless the mercy of Your Majesty protect in [. . .] will be slavery.[3] These are some of the reasons that mean this nation must perish once and for all or else free itself of the ignominies and excesses that they suffer: a foundation that [. . .] and depose a tyrannical king, a heretic and an intruder, and pay feudal loyalty to a prince [. . .] just and Catholic.

---

3. In this transcription, bracketed ellipses represent words obscured by ink stains.

Beyond the fact that the cause itself calls out to Your Majesty for protection as the sole defender of the faith, also [one should recognize] the Irish as being of legitimate Spanish blood by descent, known grounds that would seem to oblige the defense and aid [here] requested, and I doubt that there is any reason more relevant [to elicit] the generosity and piety of Your Majesty than the way in which this nation serves and has served this Catholic Crown, and with such vigor and such honesty that no prince has ever made use of Irishmen against the banners of Spain, nor has the world seen nor will histories ever recount that they have drawn their swords against the Catholic name of Your Majesty.

And in addition to these aggregated reasons, another should be added: that he who requests this help is not only a foreign knight, a prince, not only a Catholic to whom Your Majesty [would] not deny [. . .] an entire kingdom, who essentially does not ask it for himself, but for the protection of the church and the Catholic faith that, through so much vacillation, is in danger of total extinction or of allowing heresy to prevail in all those realms.

The disposition of matters and the time itself invite the execution [of this project] this very day, because [England] has no notion of them, the Scottish nobles are under arms, there is disunity among many of the English nobles, and the dissent among the titled English nobles in Ireland are much increased. One has never seen nor can one [fore]see a moment more favorable for the Irish. The prophecies of the ancient [. . .] saints [who predicted] the restoration of Ireland have now come to fruition, and [the Irish] feel that [it] is God himself who inspires them toward such a heroic enterprise.

And if Your Majesty is pleased to help such a cause, he can [do so] without any transgression to the peace arrangements with the English, because despite these [agreements], they continue to assistant Holland, France, and other enemies of Your Majesty, under dubious pretexts, and Spain can do the same, supposing that it is no less political than England. And even if they should break the [peace agreements], the advantage for Your Majesty is [worth] much more than the loss, and the gains for the English will not be so great, as we have seen in the recent wars between the Irish and the English, which required them to withdraw forces they had provided in Flanders, Holland, and other parts for their defense, through which the Catholic arms conquered many strongly fortified locations. And since

Holland today is much less powerful than it was, they will feel the loss of their assistance even more severely [in the future]. And they [the plotters] present [for the consideration] of Your Majesty that the Irish who are now in rebellion against the French are suitable for the occasion, although serious frustration [is felt] because Your Majesty did not anticipate the correspondence [of his interests] in the same effort; that nevertheless they honor the statements of the league asserting that, with present-day caution, the past loss can be remedied with eleven thousand or more infantry that Your Majesty can have [at his service] immediately, for a very moderate compensation, in case he should resolve [to accept this proposal].

And if it happens (which that kingdom will never believe) that Your Majesty for some reasons will not give his consent to the rapid acceptance of this argument and its prosecution, they propose as a means of protection for your piety, because the oppression and spiritual and corporeal risks that your kingdom would suffer are such and [involve] such circumstances, and it is proper to lose no time with the possible arrangements to escape from [this situation], that in the case of Your Majesty not accepting [the responsibility of] acting as a patron for them with your [protective] shadow and military powers, this very affliction and the severity of it has to incite them to turn to a necessary [though] disproportionate action, such as to see what other Catholic protection they may have to avail themselves of, and to put that possibility into effect. Although this, and they confess it with all their heart, would add great distress and the highest despair, and even a new lack of confidence, since for every good reason and every just confidence, they expect [these favors] only from the hand of Your Majesty, and it would be a greatly pitiable thing if—because they are rejected by Your Majesty—they should seek another shelter.

And before they should hear of so terrible a disappointment, [be assured] that they will agree to whatever conditions Your Majesty should ask, as long as they do not mean damage to those referred here. And with the pretext that you know of, it will be said that one can extract permission from the English so that an uprising in Your Majesty's name [can take place] in Ireland, and the aforesaid commanders of the league will provide up to twenty thousand infantry-men within six months and [also] for the campaign about to begin in Flanders, with moderate aid toward expenses. And in case one cannot secure the aforesaid permission, (the rebels) will search for another means, to be announced later. And because success in this matter depends, for many reasons, on quick action and because they hope to achieve the desired effect by the hand of Your Majesty without it being necessary to implore the aid, favor, and resources of any other [ruler], they propose the ways [they can be] of use to Your Majesty and the conditions they ask of you and [the manner in which all this] will be executed.

The conditions they ask of Your Majesty, followed by the proposed ways in which they will be of use:
They ask that Your Majesty send a hundred well-equipped warships within a year. And for the first wave of attacks, as many as he can, and once these ships have been delivered the sailors can be returned.

That Your Majesty order eight thousand Spaniards be sent, for the first wave of attacks on said realm, and that these solders have all [provisions] necessary for one year, after which they will be able to return [to Spain].

To be sent arms for fifty thousand men, artillery, as many musket balls, and as much gunpowder as possible and [on this] depends the winning or the losing of the realm.

That you assist said realm with a million and a half [pesos] per year, so long as the wars with the Englishman continue.

That once the English have been defeated, the Irish will become natives in the realms of Your Majesty and the Spaniards in Ireland.

That you order that the lords of this league be given a status in Spain equivalent to those they now enjoy and, in the possible event of an English victory, that [the rebel leaders] be given the same titles [as Spanish nobles].

That once the English have been defeated, Your Majesty should honor said nobles of this league with the title of duke and grandee of Spain, increasing their levels [of nobility] in each realm according to their valor and merits.

And because many titled nobles, English and Irish in Ireland, fearful of losing (through the new change) their ecclesiastical rents, which they now enjoy by inheritance, will oppose with the greatest rigor in arms not the cause, but the loss [of income] that they expect, for that reason it is proper, insofar as [these issues] touch Your Majesty, that you leave them in peaceful possession of these mentioned ecclesiastical rights provided that they obey the dictates of Your

Majesty. But if any of them come back to lack a legitimate succession in the direct male line from fathers to sons, then the aforesaid rents should revert to the church to which they were due, because in this way time and conscience will restore everything. Moreover, that the rents that today are the property of heretic ecclesiastics, [once] available and possessed [again by] that same [Catholic] church, are equal to the riches of the Catholic church in any realm.

That the titled nobility and Irish knights who have been exiled and despoiled of their estates since the last Irish wars should be returned to those same previously held estates, in case those who now hold them do not obey the voice of Your Majesty; or in the case that they do obey, then [the dispossessed] should be given other equivalent estates, or the same, so that they are given satisfaction equivalent to those who now enjoy them.

That the realm of Ireland be governed by a Council of State as a free republic and not dependent on Your Majesty, just like Venice and others, without a viceroy or any other person holding absolute command.

That Your Majesty honor [the members of] this council with the title of Highness, and when it is useful for you to make an award to some of them, that you not use the words "I command" but rather "It will please me" or "I will be served" if Your Highness does this, etc.

That, if the situation has been [well] executed, you give your assent to the presence of an Irish ambassador in the Royal Chapel, and that you will pay his expenses while he is in Spain, and the realm [of Ireland] will offer the same [honors] to your own [representatives] when they are there.

The benefits that the realm offers to Your Majesty:
That Your Majesty will have the title of Protector of Ireland.

That Your Majesty will be able to order honors at every level of rank for Spaniards with Irishmen in all the realm of Ireland according to the aforesaid mode.

That the realm of Ireland will provide assistance for the wars [of Spain] for whatever number of years and that you will be serviced by twenty thousand infantrymen, Your Majesty to contribute only 300,000 ducats to help pay expenses for each year that he may require these troops.

That Your Majesty can impose three types of taxes (however you may wish to do it) permanently on the realm of Ireland, and [the proceeds] have to be spent in that same realm on equipment for Your Majesty, and when you are no longer in need of such equipment, they must be used for the defense and protection of that same realm.

That Your Majesty can introduce the Inquisition into said realm.

That Your Majesty can request aid and donations in said realm, just as he can in Spain.

That Your Majesty can introduce the military orders of Spain into Ireland and all the ecclesiastical rents that are due in a timely manner (other than those the heretical church now enjoys, because all of them are to be transferred to Catholic [proprietorship] and will be for the use of these military orders, without the realm or republic being responsible for providing any of these land grants, but all granted only by your hand.

That said realm will refurbish, at its own cost, the fleet or galleons of the Indies at whatever time they would wish to avail themselves [of the services] of the realm.

That said realm and its natives cannot serve any other realm that might wage war with Your Majesty.

That once the islands of the Hebrides and the Orkneys that lie next to Ireland are conquered, then in case any prince or princess of Spain should marry in Ireland, they will be given [these islands] as dowry, with the title of prince [ruling] over them and other great benefits that will then be offered to them.

And if said realm at any time should break off this union with Spain or not fulfill the conditions and privileges mentioned, then Your Majesty can launch a war and take the realm by force. And, on the other hand, Ireland should have the right to oppose itself to Spain in case [Spain] should try to impose through violence more than has been agreed on.

Calculation and information relevant to carrying out the proposal:
The league for now comprises thirty-four titled nobles, who indicate to Your Majesty that they can assemble up to forty thousand men, being lords and governors of many cities, towns, and places. The titled Catholic nobles of England have six thousand additional troops ready [to participate].

The Scottish have agreed to aid them with twelve thousand infantrymen, and they themselves have forty-eight thousand men under arms for their own defense.

The priests, members of religious orders and Catholic men of letters in Ireland total five thousand who will be leaders.

Twenty thousand veteran Irish soldiers, and there are more militating in various realms who will join if called on.

Another twenty thousand expect to be sent out of the realm during these two years to [become part of] this faction.

The 8,000 men expected of Your Majesty when added to those described above come to 111,000, not including those who have not yet succumbed [to the English] within this same realm, who will add up to as much and more. Only arms, ships, and munitions for war are lacking, because there is an abundance of people. And should the Irish army [available] by sea and by land come to no more than 20,000 men, they present to Your Majesty that there would be enough force to resist and encounter the valor and force not of one realm alone but of many united. And if placed in such a situation, they will contend with any army of 200,000 united enemies and [will fight] with distinction.

The execution of the project:
Let Your Majesty command that a wise and knowledgeable person be employed for [communicating with] England, asking permission to transport all the volunteers in Ireland as intending to populate some areas of the Indies, alleging that it would be beneficial to England and its reasons of state to deport the Irish [volunteers] in this way, and said permission will certainly be given. And, when the operation begins, the aforesaid titled nobles will have their arms in hand. And Your Majesty, under the pretext of sending ships to Ireland to embark the people who have presented themselves on his behalf, can place, within those very ships, the supplies that are requested by those who stand with the Earl of Tyrone, a person very important to the Irish because of the name of his father and the fear that the English have of him. And with both powers joining together in Ireland, one can expect that the intentions will result in a supremely felicitous victory. And while the enemies are defeated through this impetus, the native inhabitants who are spread out through many realms and the promised supplies will punctually arrive.

In case Your Majesty has [present] need of the aforesaid men who have to be raised for the present occasion, it would be necessary to postpone the execution [of the plan of] this faction already discussed until the following year, and then [those troops] can be made use of in that manner.

Document 2: Proclamation of Insurrection for the
Kingdom of New Spain

William Lamport died at the stake in Mexico City because he had
defied the Inquisition and attempted to incite a revolutionary
movement in New Spain itself, designed to separate New Spain from
the Spanish Crown and emancipate the indigenous people, African
slaves, and people of mixed race. When he was arrested in 1642, the
Inquisition seized his personal papers. Among them they found this
proclamation, with which they could then brand him as a fomenter of
sedition.

In the days of the conquest, indigenous thinkers and Spanish
humanists discussed the legitimacy of the Spanish dominion in
Hispanic America. It was a subject that would not be raised again
until three centuries later, with the movement toward independence
in Mexico, and it would be a piecemeal and gradual process. In the
midst of this ocean of time, Lamport had the distinction of openly
discussing the legitimacy of Spanish rule when no other thinkers were considering the matter. He also imagined a new regime
where the indigenous nobility would be elevated to the same rank
as the Spanish, the African slaves would be emancipated, and there
would be "equal opportunity" for all, an idea that would reappear
in nineteenth-century ideologies of independence. He conceived of
an insurrection with possible international ramifications, and he
planned to implement it with a no-nonsense system of punishments
and incentives for the various groups involved. The document has
no title, and we have given it a provisional one: "Proclamation of

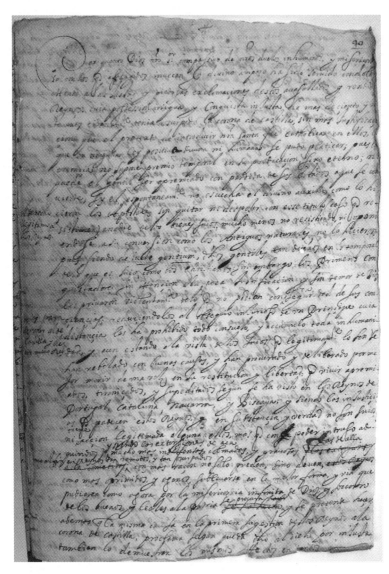

FIG. 3 First page of the "Proclamation of Insurrection for the Kingdom of New Spain." ITESM, fol. 40r.

Insurrection for the Kingdom of New Spain."[1] It establishes this Irishman as an extremely early precursor of Mexican independence.

How[2] our Lord God has been treated with deceit, he who has compassion for our inhuman sufferings and is merciful to the afflicted who invoke his divine protection, [and who is] attentive to the just and pious outcries of these subjugated and surrendered realms, the unjust conquest and iniquitous possession of which the Crown of Castile has for more than 120 years tyrannically usurped, with no more justification than the pretext of introducing our holy Catholic faith, which could not be put into practice according to any positive divine or human law, because belief does not suppose a temporal prize in the preaching of it but rather an eternal prize, nor can the heathen be pressured with the loss of his estates so that he may convert, if he does not spontaneously hear [and accept] the divine consolations [of religion], as did the apostles without depriving or despoiling them, with this excuse, of any of their possessions (should they resist) and much less so if they neither resist nor oppose conversion as the ancient natives did, because according to the [Roman] law of nations (*iure gentium*), said heathens are owners in the temporal sphere of what belongs to them, just like Christians. Nevertheless, the first conquistadors, attending neither to the paucity of justification nor to the fear of God, deprived them violently of what they could not [justifiably deprive them of], with little conscientious conviction, reducing [their possessions and themselves] to an injurious donation to a prince whose distance from them has deprived them of any consolation and accumulated every kind of inhumanity. And still contemplating their possessions (which legitimately belong to them), they have rebelled for good reason and have endeavored and decided that it is better to die at once [in pursuit of] restitution and liberty than to live under pressure, tyrannized and crushed, as has been demonstrated [by the rebellions] in the realms of Portugal, Catalonia, Navarre, and Biscay.

1. "Proclamation of Insurrection," ITESM, fols. 40r–47v. The paleography is by Larisa González (Biblioteca del Tecnólogico de Monterrey) and Andrea Martínez Baracs; the orthography and punctuation are normalized.
2. Written in the left margin: "the illegitimate right to said realms / causes for deposing him of Castile and electing a new king."

And given the injustices that these realms endure, which in substance and in truth do not belong (to the conquistadors), who neither have any legitimate [right] over them, no more than what has been acquired through intrusive power, and therefore the extortions from this [American] side [of the ocean] are much more indefensible, overweening, and onerous [than] those in Europe, [taking place] after all in realms so remote and usurped to such a degree, with more reason they not only can but should, being so heavily oppressed and estranged, rebel in the best way and form that they are able to, just as now, through the infinite mercy of God and as help for those who are good and loyal to the fatherland, they endeavor and are attempting to do. Beyond the fact that the very reason for the original subjection of these realms to the Crown of Castile proclaims its injustice to heaven, this is also demonstrated by very wasteful activities[3] throughout so many years, because so many treasures that the kings involved have acquired until this day, so many achievements and interests that those involved have usurped, entailing so many risks, so many rents, vassals, possessions of the first conquistadors, and to what end? What realms? What prosperities have we seen achieved according to the just judgments of God? Not a single one! Far from it! These aforementioned conquistadors go begging, passively acceptant of the viceroy providing them with the humblest judiciary office there may be in these realms so that they may not die of hunger. And even this they will not achieve. The fleets are oft-times lost, and when they have reached Spain, foreign realms are more the masters [of their wealth] than the Spaniards who were supposed to have benefited from them. And the world is witness to this. Nor do the sons come to enjoy what the fathers have heretofore strived for, because [these possessions were] violently usurped from their rightful owners.

And[4] to these reasons another is to be added, of no less efficacy or evidential worth: and it is that, for the same tyrannically possessed (seizures), not only the kings of Castile but the aforementioned

3. Written in the left margin: "Facts that declare the illegitimacy / Those who possess these realms live excommunicated / To ask absolution from His Holiness / Any knight can legitimately undertake to liberate the realm."

4. Written in the left margin: "Even though the kings firmly possess these realms, they can be taken away from them and even should be, and why? / A true and secure election and a legitimate / painful state of the ecclesiastics / New reasons for a new election. / The priests sold [to the highest bidder]."

conquerors and residents of these realms have necessarily incurred the excommunication of heaven [. . .] even though it was not expressly sent down on them, at least tacitly they fell under the kind of censure reserved for those who usurp, steal, or keep possession of what is not theirs against the will of [its real] owners. And, furthermore, there is hardly a person in these kingdoms who do not live, by himself and in general, excommunicated by his own actions, as withholders of goods and sacrilege, stolen property or debts [. . .], so that every day they fall under these censures, without, in general, any kind of scruple about restitution.

Beyond what has been argued [already], [there is more] because of the execrable violence of the viceroys and their insolent threats, and consequently of ordinary people and their followers, in opposing the holy archbishops and daring to violate feudal privileges and the immunities of churches, with the most complete irreverence and disrespect for God and his church and the holy ministers.

Because of which causes and motives, it will be necessary that we turn then to his Holiness [the pope], as his faithful and obedient children, giving him on the one hand due obedience, and on the other imploring him to absolve us of these censures and excommunications in general and throughout the realm, so that being in the grace and favor of God, all our monarchy and achievements will have a happy conclusion and the finest spirit.

With the tyrannical and unjust possession by the Crown of Castile now established and its brittle, intrusive conduct in these realms, [it is] a more than urgent reason for some zealous knight to execute its restoration and restitution and to entrust those who have a vote to, of their own free will, elect him who will govern them in peace and defend them in war and award them honors in both [circumstances] as their prince.

And also there are other grounds, some nearly as important and others even more so, that create an obligation for all to depose the kings of Castile from [ruling in] these realms, who never were nor will they ever be accepted as legitimate possessors of these [realms], not even if someone were to undertake the same procedure as we are now undertaking, because always, in more matters, whatever apparent procedure they might make would be seen as a violent [act]. And it is certain that if the naturales of the realms, if they were allowed to choose anew who should or should not be their king, they would [merely] resort to another [like the previous] and [gain only] a new subjection, such that the injustice will remain. Which in our case [would not be so], because, through the consent of those very naturales who are the only people as proprietaries with a vote of substance in this election—[the rights of] all others are [merely] incidental, secondary—we will be elected with total fairness and untampered-with general consent, giving us possession and dominion as thanks for restoring their liberty and ancient rights.

Beyond the reasons [already] related and so obviously antithetical to the present retention of these realms by the Crown of Spain, [there are] other absurdities such that any one of them is sufficient justification for annulling that right, [if the king] ever had it. For those miserable vassals live reduced to so mortal a pain of servitude that the most free among them appears most captive, embroiled in so many persecutions and subject to so many calamities [stemming from] greed, honor, authority, and [their specific] grievances.

Let us consider the case of the holy priests and members of religious orders as both greatly offended and wretched, since they lack the rewards their learning, merit, lineage, and holiness deserve, on the one hand because of distance (from power), on the other because of the profit making and simony to which they are subject, against [all] positive human and divine right, in the provision of ecclesiastical honors without concern for merits, to which one must add the universal feeling among those of noble blood, acquired virtue, and eminent learning, who see themselves defrauded of what in all fairness belongs to them; and even those who do gain honors despair at times of that which they have achieved through such zealous application of time and of money, for the great delay in the court of Spain and the necessary wait for confirmation and honors from His Holiness [the pope], which is now being remedied since, only through official approval from His Holiness and our own appointment, can one arrive at decisions befitting the merits and quality of each individual.

The laypersons and the conquistadors are completely exhausted and [reduced to] beggars, with their exploits neither noted, prized, nor honored, [as well as being] oppressed by the most despicable profiteers, meaning a loss in wealth and profit, with neither nobility nor virtue receiving the protection that heaven and Spanish policies[5]

5. Written in the left margin: "The rare benefits of our forces continue."

require. The republicans are wasting away in the midst of disastrous hardships, since trade with other kingdoms is impeded by embargos, contraband regulations, and capital punishments and closed off unless [the trade] is with Spain, to which they are necessarily obliged, and the same necessity constrains them to buy for 1,000 [pesos] that which is barely worth 1. Given that they are deprived of any consolation, even were these misfortunes limited to these vexations and tyrannies, they would be more tolerable if the small amount of trade allowed were not loaded down with so many duties of taxes, tributes, interior sales taxes, and thousands of other difficulties, given how reduced the people are to hunger and a lack of basic provisions that now they are desperately gasping [for breath], mute and stunned amid their piteous sufferings. Justice and posts of honor within the republic are put up for auction and sold (a tyranny never previously seen or heard), with the pure, upright, and meritorious vassal stripped of what the laws and the republic itself had established as his reward and had agreed that the kings of Castile, as administrators, should divide among the meritorious not as their own (property) but common to all, with the understanding that one does not reduce to tyranny that which was [formerly] in accordance with justice.

And also the courts, because of [over]tolerance and arrogance and because of the profiteering and greed of some ministers among them, have been reduced throughout these realms to confusion, bribery, and intolerable [abuse of] power, without the poor man or the destitute attaining any consolation, because only the powerful man is protected: robbery, evil, vice, and sacrilege [are] defended, and if the thievery is not significant enough for the stolen goods to be squandered, he dies not because of what he stole but of how little, because there was not enough to divide among the judges involved.

The innocent are placed in prison, forced to flee, let unsupported, and subject to harassment. Passion in the form of Christianity and [the accompanying] zeal are diminished. Neither compensation nor justice [is forthcoming] against those who govern but allow no recourse for appeal [against them], because even if a complaint reaches [its destination], [nevertheless] before that grievance is heard [or] after the suffering is substantiated, bribery is always there as a way out. The whole realm is inundated with taxes, wasted money, interior sales taxes, and vices. Everything is confusion, burning, uproar, tyranny, and impious cruelty. Each fleet [that lands here] results in exorbitant hemorrhages of 20 million, 18 million, or at least 15 million [reales] from these realms to Spain, leaving the one hollow and the other in no way improved. If such extensive wealth were kept here, even if it may be late [to do so], we would be among the most powerful in the world, for if commerce among nations were allowed to be free, there would be more than enough galleons and other [types of vessels]. There is little we lack, given that wine, olive oil, and other odds are more abundant in these realms than in any other. The [production] of silks will increase once trade with Spain is annulled and once those who have no work apply themselves to [producing] this and other infinite kinds of merchandise currently forbidden by Spain.

Moreover, it will be necessary that China actively maintain its commerce, since Castile is more interested in it than we are, because of the silver and the supply of gunpowder and munitions, with which Spain pays for the silks of China. Furthermore, we will order the construction of ships for travel to Chinese cities not tied to Castile, and the success and profit will be doubled and, if they deny us that commerce, [it will result in] the total ruin of the Philippines. And if this happens, even our public streets will be awash with silver and riches. And for our support and defense, we alone, through divine assistance, are sufficient against the power of the world, without the aid of any other [nation] of Europe. And if the ruler of Castile should attempt to repeat his unjust intention to take back these realms, the rulers of France, England, and Portugal, merely to be allowed free access to trade, will come to our aid when they notice any slight movement on the part of Spain. The same is true of Venice and Holland, with whom we will be able to enter into a trusting coexistence. And even if all were to refuse to help us (which would be impossible), our own so thoroughly united forces would, with only three fortresses, defend us against the greater part of the wide world.

And what has very much contributed to the utterly ruinous state of affairs until now are the outcries, complaints, and tears from these poor naturales, caciques, and principals, as well as republicans and commoners, who live not only deprived of their means of support, possessions, and land but miserably tyrannized and condemned to forced-labor gangs as if they were not free men, but slaves of the slaves themselves, who also lord it over them, and liable to feudal requirements and despicable tributes, obligating them, by means of force and without any payment whatever for the labor of their bodies, to serve perpetually in mines, at various labors, on drainage projects, on plantations, in sugar mills, without allowing them to become masters of that which belongs to them alone. What a grievous thing such tyranny is, with more than two hundred million of them having died and been consumed since the conquest, which no devout heart could hear of without being moved to great distress, given that all reason suggests that they are the masters here, at least as much, if not more, than us, since the realm is theirs.

The same affliction and pain results from the tyrannous enslavement of so great a number of Negroes, mulattoes, Berbers, and other infinite [racial] branches, whose natural rights are usurped by the Spaniards, with little fear of God, because from the state of freedom in which they were raised, the Spaniards reduce them to miserable slavery, servitude, and the most wretched of sufferings, since it forecloses their liberty, the sweetest and most desirable thing in this whole life, ranking them on a par in estimation and mistreatment with brute animals;[6] [even though] they are created and redeemed—and capable of the same glory as we are—and, as both Christians and Catholic members of the church, deprived of that which is more estimable than living, and that is liberty. And this forcefully calls on and stirs divine piety to show mercy for their serious and long-standing affliction and servitude, [and to show] pity for so much exertion [and to] mitigate so many and such overwhelming grievances, [and ultimately to] free these kingdoms and vassals from these and other infinite tyrannies such as now are planned and being carried out.

Therefore, our Lord God, by whose hand and infinite power princes are chosen and kings named with no consideration for lineages or ancestral lines, but [only] according to his incomprehensible mysteries, since among the ethnics and heathens we have living examples of this very thing, only through the morality of one's actions could earthbound (not eternal) power be obtained. Did not Pertinax ascend from a slave to the good fortune of emperor? Did not Marinus and Maximus gain the scepter, although they were blacksmiths? Was not Philip an emperor, having been previously [. . .] of the plow? Did not the coarse but valiant emperors Aurelius,

6. Written in the left margin: "So many emperors of low descent / Claims his blood to be royal and declares himself son of the Most Serene King Philip."

Maximinus, and Hercules elevate themselves to become emperors? Valentinian and Valens, sons of a rope-making father, did they not rule over the Roman Empire? Were not Justin and Justinian, two cattle herders, masters of the diadem? Mauritius and Theodoric, the one a notary, the latter a shopkeeper? Isauricus, Traulus, Basileus, Macedonius, all of humble origin but lords of the world for their virtue and proper governing? And countless others.

Even such heroic blood as the kings now emblazon [on their heraldic crests] did not run through us; this would be of little importance, so long as heaven with its powerful hand and our own virtue might arrive at the wished-for remedy. So much the more as having (which we do have) the most royal blood of the kings of Europe in our veins on both paternal and maternal sides, being the reputed son of the heroic and illustrious barons of Wexford, whose royal ancestry descends from the kings of the Goths, Longbards, and Iberians, from princes ruling in Biscay. I am though truly the son of the Most Serene Prince and Lord Philip III, who is with God, and of the illustrious lady, the Countess of Riff, who visited the court with her husband the baron, who in the year 1613 led—at his own expense—a thousand Irish infantrymen to Spain and passed on with them to Flanders, where, while returning to Madrid with his spouse, God was pleased, on that road, to take the baron to himself, having been formerly married to the illustrious lady, the Countess of Media, leaving my mother in her young years and of rare beauty, to arrive at the court as a widow and asking permission to return to her native land. His Majesty the king my master was enamored of her beauty, with such honest modesty that it was never known how finally the love of such princes [was consummated] except as a great secret.

From this close connection I was born, a year and a half after the death of the baron who was considered to be my father, when [my mother] for the honor that was gestating [within her] left Spain and gave birth in Ireland, receiving amorous messages every two months from His Majesty, greatly favoring the person of his son, who with tenderness he desired to see, saying that if by chance God should take him away before I had already reached an age when he could see me, he would very much entrust my person and communicate it in secret (as in effect he did) to his son the prince, who became King Philip IV, so that he might learn of his brotherhood and obligation and should hold me in equal respect with the rest of his brothers, attending to the royal and illustrious blood not only of my father but also of my mother.

And when I was five years old, God was pleased to take unto himself the king, my lord, and when I reached the age of nine, my mother and lady sent me to other kingdoms (as was the usage and custom with great lords) in order to learn various languages. And my brother, King Philip IV, asked in complete secrecy that I should be sent to Spain to conform with what the king, his father, had communicated to him during his final illness. In keeping with that [decision], I passed through France and took a ship from the city of Saint-Malo, [and] an enemy pirate captured me, and coming to know, by some means, who I was at least on my mother's side through information from the crew of the ship, he made me a general of his four galleons, when I was fourteen years old or somewhat less. And I spent two and a half years in this kind of compulsory life till I brought them to the service of the Crown of Spain in the port of Deán in the Kingdom of Galicia and conveyed them to the Holy Office of the Inquisition in Santiago, [and] they were absolved of their heresies (those who practiced them), with myself serving as an interpreter to confess them and in, in person, teach them the Christian doctrine, and they were 452 persons, and four galleons with thirty-two pieces of artillery on each ship.

And His Majesty knew who the person in question, namely myself, really was, though I was ignorant of this until the year 1632, when my mother and lady sent me to speak with my uncle, the prince of Vetonia, when I was already an advanced student at the royal and miraculous [college of] San Lorenzo, having been earlier [a student] among the noble children who wear the habit of Christ. [The prince of Vetonia] ordered me to maintain total discretion, that I was to keep my secret until the king, my brother, should divulge it, with the favors that he began to do for me, as he was done up to the present moment when he gave me the letters of my mother and lady, with some of them [expressly] for her, in accordance with [the instructions of] my father, the king, which now are in the keeping of my uncle, the prince of Vetonia, who is a member of His Highness's Council of War and holds the golden key of [those who wear] the habit of Calatrava, knight-commander of Carrión, majordomo of His

Majesty, and field commander of the Irish contingent at[7] Fuenterrabía and other [battles]. And His Majesty, recognizing the means
at my disposal or to place me at the risk of fortune, sent me out of
my college to accompany the cardinal-infante to Flanders, given my
study and experience in the matters of fortification and squadrons.
I obeyed and, proceeding from Milan and [. . .] of my brother the
infante, not through any awareness of our parentage but because of
a natural sympathy between the two of us and our similarity in all
things and also because my talents contributed to his honoring me
when I was lacking in other titles. We arrived at Norlenga, where the
enemy king of Sweden awaited us with the confederated heretics of
Germany. The king of Hungary and the emperor of Germany joined
with us. And when I was preparing for battle that day, I arranged the
squadron with [the participation of] Father Gamoso of the Society of
Jesus, who was my teacher in mathematics, as a result of which we
went on to win the most celebrated victory ever achieved or heard-of,
killing twenty-two thousand enemies and losing [only] two hundred
men. Upon my return to Spain, even before I arrived, His Majesty
sent me an order to travel, with an embassy, to Venice. I obeyed [. . .]
did not [. . .] me as a young man. I returned; they gave me [the honor
of official] state papers and the favor of the count-duke.

I performed prodigious services in secret matters of state, raised
two hundred infantrymen at my own expense, went to Fuenterabbía
at my own expense, entered with the first relief force of two hundred men, being surrounded by twenty-seven thousand enemies. I
led assaults; I assisted in everything; I returned to court; I received
(among many other embassies [I was assigned] to hear by order of
His Majesty) the embassy of the princes and Catholic nobles of Ireland, asking for His Majesty's assistance in throwing off the tyrannical yoke of the English, having seen the opportunity fortunately
[offered by] the rebellion of Scotland. Two members of each council
met together over the issue, which was divulged in general [only]
as a great secret. They did not know how to resolve so difficult an
undertaking; the king was distressed, and I requested that I alone be

7. Written in the left margin: "true . . . Accompanies the cardinal-infante to Flan-
ders. Battle of Norlenga. Embassy to Venice. Serves in the state with the count-duke.
Enters Fuenterabbía and other matters. Receives embassies. Arranges the Irish faction.
Just complaint against the king."

sent [to parlay], which was done. I arranged the matter in a manner
equally agreeable to both realms, and since [the Irish] happened to act
before the political instructions [were settled], they rose in rebellion
without assistance from the king. Then [. . .] made me [. . .] expanded
with two titles of field commander and many other [. . .] as well as
[such recognition as] the insignia [marking the] title of captain and
granting me expenses, status, and considerable terms, and so on. And
I was to go out personally to raise 2,400 Irishmen, who would be
readied in secret.

His Majesty suspended my departure and, instead of finally
revealing my [real] person—at this point I would not have deserved
it for my blood [alone] but for such portentous [exploits] in my
younger years—he exiled me from those kingdoms, following the
reasons of state of the count-duke, under the pretext that the Marquis of Cadereyta had informed him of this city [of Mexico] being in
rebellion and that my person was of great importance for what was
happening,[8] [though I was to maintain] complete secrecy, without
anyone knowing of it, and that I should travel here as if I were any
other coach traveler with the dissimulation and caution suitable to
[having being sent on] the recommendation of His Majesty, with
two objectives, the one to gain information on the state of affairs at
that time, the second [to seek information] on the conduct and rule
of the Marquis of Villena. And all this was no more than a pretext to
confuse me so that I might not come to recognize my equal [lofty]
status, nor did I have occasion for anyone to tell me of it, since they
feared the acclaim [I had received], my exploits, my achievements,
my talents in matters of state, my military guile, and that all of it
together with the loftiness of my blood could work toward some
disorder, and more [than that even] since I had suffered such notable grievances in being deprived for so many years of the privileges
and greatness that belonged to me. And all this because of the whim
and caprice of only two men. As the prince Sigismundo had suffered
before at his father's hand, a credulous believer in the stars, [whose
forebodings] were verified when [his son] avenged himself upon him,
overthrowing him, and taking his realm from him in just compensation for the damage done to him, for [his father] had denied him

---

8. Written in left margin: "The king's reasons of state for exiling me / example
. . . of epilogue . . . just and painful complaint."

the [chance to be] the person he himself had made him, since it had been foretold that he was to overthrow [his father] and bring him to his knees. And if the father had not offered him the chance, the son would never have carried this out.

So the king and the count-duke [acted] according to the shifting and inconstant exigencies of state, and I, on the other hand, being patient, long-suffering, and dissembling to the point that heaven took pity on my treatment and the wrong done to me. Never had I made myself known as anyone but the person identified in the information furnished to His Majesty when I entered the colleges already mentioned.

After I arrived in these kingdoms, without His Majesty taking note of my always so obedient toils, nor even concerning himself with clothing or feeding me and much less my outward appearance, which, both in his opinion and in mine, is at odds with my employment, I have suffered the most terrible troubles that I will not say a prince has suffered but the most battered slave, without daring to complain or announce my penurious state to anyone, nor even to make myself known any more than my natural merits proclaim, and [even] this to very few, because all admire my well-known talents, with myself little rewarded. But if the count intended me to walk in the steps of his Don Julián,[9] he is very deluded and ought to know the great difference between a prince and an uncouth vassal, who was conceived by another vassal and a low-born married woman, and himself married to another woman of his same status but divorced

9. Don Enrique Felípez de Guzmán was the name that, in the absence of a legitimate descendant, the count-duke wished to give this son of his, who was also called Don Julián de Valcárcel. He was brought up by a couple who were relatives of the count-duke, under the protection of a Valcárcel, whose name he took. We regret to find that his career was somewhat similar to Lamport's, though without any distinction: he was page to an archbishop relative; went to Spanish America, where he was nearly taken to prison; enlisted on his return; and claimed to have served in Italy and Flanders before returning to court in 1639. While there he hastily married the daughter of a royal clerk. The historian John Elliott calls him a "wastrel." The count-duke forced the young couple to divorce and announced that Julián was his son in 1641—at the time of the outbreak of the scandal that accelerated his downfall. The Duke of Medina Sidonia, a relative of his—head of the main branch of the House of Guzmán—was accused of being a traitor; of having supported his brother-in-law, the Duke of Braganza, now king of Portugal; and of participating, with the support of France and the Low Countries, in a conspiracy to be proclaimed "King of Andalusia and the Indies." Here too is an echo of Lamport's conspiratorial career. Elliott, *Count-Duke of Olivares*, 618–19.

unfairly by he who rules and if he dares let him bury me and even (leave me) as oppressed and even dead like Don Carlos[10] because[11] I was worthy of my good fortune and my blood, which is so valiantly hid [in spite of] my own distress and the injustices dealt [me] by that tyrant, and my brother the king (an equally uncaring tyrant) did not remedy [the situation] even though he could and should have, before [. . .] offensive to his grandeur and [. . .] to his person, with me having been so complaisant while in his service, as though I had been born with no obligations other than to please him. Here is the universal downfall of all: over and over I ask you vassals to take pity not on me—though the same cause requires it of you—but on yourself, who run the same risks and share the same dangers.

And at once I had reported on the peaceable state of these realms and on the offense done to the very loyal vassals in the sinister report produced by the Marquis of Cadereyta, in the hope that the king would show his gratitude to these realms by honoring them; he provided merely a letter [expressing] consolation and satisfaction at the secure situation [of these realms], which clearly would be a cause, I would not say for distress but rather constant despair for all. In accordance with the love I have for these peaceful and generous vassals, and because I naturally find tyranny, injustice, and unspeakable acts abhorrent, I reported, with all vigor and in no uncertain terms, on the ill-timed rule of the Marquis of Villena. I fulfilled the intentions that I had weighed within the politics of my own reasoning of state, based always on the justification of wholesome reasons and intentions, judging on the one hand that the government should be dismissed, on the other that since he in power was selling such a large number of patronages, it would be very difficult to establish my intentions and your [my future vassals'] prospects of relief. Because it appears, in line with his previous attitudes, that he was

10. King Philip IV, having no male descendants, would have his younger brother Charles as his heir. Charles and the next youngest brother, Ferdinand, with whom Lamport traveled to Flanders, were the object of intrigues stirred up by the count-duke, who wanted to create a division between them and the king, above all when the king fell gravely ill in 1627, and the succession became a pressing issue. Charles died in 1632, at the age of twenty-five. We can clearly see in this passage that Lamport was outspoken in his criticism of his supposed protector, the Count-Duke of Olivares.

11. Written in the left margin: "Remedy, the little love that His Majesty shows toward these kingdoms / refute the provision of the Marquis of Villena / Persuasive reasons for the disillusionments of the vassals."

inclined to act expeditiously [in the launching of a rebellion], even if he would not [possess] the zest, valor, prudence, or [good] counsel to undertake so difficult and arduous an affair, like someone who was unaware, on the one hand, of the actions of Castile [in relation] to these deprivations, and on the other hand as someone more honored than aggrieved with the maintenance of this government. And since it pained me that he so afflicted the vassals of these realms, and he did not have the capacity for immediate action (which is implicit in my blood), but rather it may perhaps be because the absence of his son made him a coward and also the suspicion that he would lose his estates, in which case his word would not accomplish what the heavens had saved for me [alone].

Given this, you now see that each one of the new viceroys, like the limited people [they are], tries to ingratiate himself with my brother by going on tyrannizing you, and each day your greatness will be [steadily] diminished, and the more you postpone your own freedom, the closer you come to the precipice. And although in the last communication that the king wrote to me in his own handwriting and also in the penultimate [communication], and also [in the communication from] the count-duke and his secretary[12] Pedro López de Calo in response to my earlier letters and in conformity with new events about which they informed me—either to encourage me to live on as an exile or to further dazzle and disorient me—[they stated] that I had been made Marquis of Cropani, an Italian title of nobility surviving from the royal establishments, a position for someone [seemingly] not born to that level, yet [someone] better than the infante Don Juan de Austria and with much greater advantages on the maternal side, equal in the end to the princesses of the highest degree. Then does not this same gift serve as a greater affront and offence to me and a greater spray of venom [than is] displayed by our very powerful enemies?

In consequence of which, heaven was pleased to inspire to my energies and give me the force and vigor and prudence to conceal [my reaction to] such atrocious offenses, until this moment in which, by divine and sovereign impulse and through celestial means and

12. Written in the left margin: "They made me Marquis of Cropani and super-intendent of the royal establishments / Sublime resolution / Declaration to our Lord God / To the Holy Office of the Inquisition."

assistance, I am ready to take up arms and with them (by the most peaceful and merciful means possible) shake off the heavy yoke and the tyranny that these realms endure, freeing every sort of oppressed [people] and relieving all of whatever oppression they endure, in the form and manner and with the qualities and privileges that follow.

And because it is better, before all things, to firmly base our good intentions on God, we claim to live and die in the holy Catholic faith of our Lord Jesus Christ, truly [born] a man, offering our necks, with all reverence, to the gentle yoke of his sacrosanct law professed by the Roman Catholic apostolic holy mother church. And in his name, we render our dutiful obedience to his deputy, our most holy father Urban the Eighth, Pontifex Maximus, may God keep him safe, according to the way and in the manner of our most Catholic predecessors across so many centuries, including similar reverence in this respect to the Holy Office of the Inquisition, confirming and corroborating its holy institution forever and ever in these realms, to whose holy tribunal we will make a solemn vow, in the name of the church, to defend the holy Catholic faith unto death in all our realms. And our successors must do the same, on pain of their kingdoms and hereditary rights being taken from them through a free election [and] the common acclaim of all.

For our second point, because we judge (and it is true) that for us and our heirs to have legitimate possession [of these kingdoms] and for our legitimacy to be unarguable, we must conquer and liberate these kingdoms and vassals by force of arms, which [once] reduced to a peaceful union and vassals [. . .]¹³ complete and secure, we intend to call a meeting of town authorities so that, since it will be seen as convenient and necessary, in remuneration and as a reward for our work and attending to our valor, that they chose us for their king and prince as well as our successors, or what seems best to them, with the provision that in these courts, the naturales and the freedmen will have voice and vote, just like the Spaniards.

13. Written in the left margin: "Declaration to the kingdom / Edicts favorable to all these kingdoms / There will be no taxes or tributes / The administrators will be free [of taxes] / that even in these matters we can agree that no one better [than I am], taking into account our long and still active experience in government business, for greater success in everything, I desire that there be consent and communication among all the interested parties themselves, because necessarily they will consider it with the same zeal and will vote on it with the same energy."

The third point: We make it known to all that we immediately order that it be divulged (and we so divulge it) that from now on all these kingdoms of greater America (and those bordering them) are dismembered and separated from the Crown of Castile without obeying any other prince than he . . .[14] under penalty of incurring vociferous resentment. And in line with this present [announcement] we order revoked and we do revoke and annul every kind of tax, tribute, interior transit tax, and any new impositions, leaving to the will of all [the establishment of] a new, gentle, and moderate order of royal rights for the general defense of all and the splendor of their prince, and for now the royal tribute and the funds remaining from it (should be) available for the defense of all.

Additionally, we absolve this city of Mexico (provided that the city does not oppose itself to [the gaining of] its freedom) from any kind of debt that it has incurred or should incur, the city itself along with its individuals and suppliers, and let them continue without any increase, unless they be taxes, from which we have relieved them forever and ever. Let commerce be free and without [restrictive] taxation, in the form mentioned. Let everything that is not burdensome go on in the usual manner, tithes or the fifth part of the production of mines and that which the Commercial Council and the city with the name of the kingdom should judge to be proper, urging that they be very moderate. And should the Commercial Council and the city also promulgate laws of good contract and government and [determine] with which nations it is useful to do so? And it is to be greatly desired that they name and put forward ambassadors to Rome, France, Venice, Holland, Portugal, and Ireland. The tributes of the naturales should immediately be suspended and for the rest who are involved there should be no work levies, but let them not stop working to sustain themselves and the republic, they just as much as the Spaniards and other people, under pain of our indignation and punishment. And those who have a dependence on Spain for their commerce and interchanges, let them continue it in the best way they can, in cases where it is necessary and advantageous, so as not to defraud anyone or be defrauded. But there should be no one who can actually receive a cargo from there, nor send any either; any

14. Here is a gap left in the sentence from crossing out "who would be elected at the (proper) time."

such activity must be by way of exchanges alone. And this will have to be done through other nations who make agreements with us or through wealthy individuals so that there is no dearth of mutual restitution.

The fourth point: Let as many slaves as will rise in rebellion within these kingdoms at once be freed so as to defend and liberate themselves, and without excluding any condition or quality, whether they be African or of mixed race. Thenceforward and in conformity with their services and deeds, they will be as capable of receiving awards, titles of nobility, land grants, holy orders, lordships, and official positions on land and sea, in the republic as well as the government, as Spaniards themselves, and the rest of them, who apply themselves to cultivating the earth and being laborers, in conformity with their talent and application, should be given whatever they need, making them their own masters and free [of slavery].

The sixth point:[15] That the Spaniards, who will promptly, with their persons, their retinues, and their slaves, come forward to strengthen and defend their freedom, will not only remain in possession of the estates, wealth, and possessions that they have now—although said slaves will be liberated by our edict and their own valor—but they will have to be given not only satisfaction equal to their now freed slaves but much more as well, beyond the rewards that these Spaniards may deserve, in whatever specific object or form they may request.

The seventh point: That the slaves and even the free men of their kind who do not take up arms at that moment for the call to liberty will forever after [be slaves]—they, their sons, their descendants, and posterity, without there being any ransom or cause in a will that can liberate them, and we and our successors will continue to buy them, using them in the mines, textile factories, forced labors, agriculture, and other servile tasks, paying us through their personal labor, and they will be left to our successors as a royal possession linked to the entailed property of the Crown.

The eighth point: The Spaniards, of whatever rank they may be, who not only fail to oppose but do not personally support acts that, when the time comes, would lead to this justified liberty for all, will

---

15. There is no point 5. Further on another error was corrected by us—point 10 in place of point 12—in the manuscript, which is, we should remember, only a draft.

be considered and have the repute of vile people and be dispossessed of whatever wealth, posts, dignities, special exemptions, or privileges they hold and be considered incapable of any reward (as they themselves now consider slaves) and their sons and descendants will be considered unworthy of any right to reward or positions and will always be driven out to the Chichimec frontiers, since they are opposed to their own improvement and liberty, and they will be immediately placed on a list so that they [become] well-known enemies of God and his grandeur.

The ninth point: The Spaniards who, with their people and retinue, stepped forward and became part [of the rebellion] and helped with this holy conspiracy and universal liberation, beyond the fact that they will retain the peaceful possession of all they now enjoy and possess, at the same time they will augment their estates and dignities according to the merits of each, with titles of counts, barons, marquises, dukes, knights, and other honorific and beneficial dignities, giving them villages, rents, and royal land grants, offices, or preeminence in order to expand the renown of each one, according to his dictates and obligations.

The tenth point: That all posts, offices, or dignities provided by the king of Castile should continue in their current form, with their [same] force and vigor, for the same length of time and [with the same] date of completion as when they were granted and with the same special privileges, provided that they do not oppose the intent and [the objective of] freedom, nor do they give aid [to the pro-Spanish forces] should the occasion arise. And if any post or office is eliminated, such as those tax collectors, eliminated because there are no taxpayers [in their area of concern], another more honorable and personally rewarding position will be given to them.

The eleventh point: The Spaniards who were at the beginning of [the action of] this political faction and the liberated and free naturales who were without any kind of wealth and were poor will be masters with equal shares of all the economic resources, mobile as well as fixed, of those who opposed them, and of their public offices, and they and all their descendants will be considered nobles and hidalgos of lineage forever and ever, and, provided there is no opposition, they will be rewarded liberally to their content and our satisfaction.

The twelfth point: The naturales who establish that they have been defrauded of their means of subsistence from the conquest till this very day will have their rights restored to them, and those who show themselves loyal and desirous of their liberty will be rewarded, and the caciques, nobles, and knights among them who with their own persons, their followers, and their estates would assist and further this enterprise should be rewarded with titles of marquises, dukes, counts, barons, holy orders, grandees of the kingdom, and other favors, conforming to the merits of each, with the same privileges and precedence as the Spaniards and able to display carriages, liveries, arms, and more, without exception.

The thirteenth point: The same with the other classes of people, of whatever quality or condition they may be, without there being for anyone in the future any inequality in the matter of being capable of merited reward, as we have said, for all men are free from now on and the offspring of their own exploits and as capable as the Spaniards of ecclesiastical as well as secular and military achievement.

The fourteenth point: Because serious confusion [would] follow for the republic due to the necessary but very quickly accomplished freeing of the slaves and much damage to the vassals who have placed their hopes and remedies for everything on their haciendas, sugarcane mills, textile factories, and other employments and would suffer from the absence of those who manage, work, and invigorate these activities and therefore will necessarily feel serious distress at what will appear to them as the loss of their slaves, we order that the aforementioned masters of haciendas, shops, textiles factories, forced labors, or the supervisors of officials should at that point begin to pay [the freed slaves] for their personal work as [befitting] the free men they are, [and the freedmen] will then help them out, without anyone daring to injure them, to whip them, no other action than to dismiss them if they do not perform adequately, just as would be done in the end with the Spaniards. And the masters who should demonstrate, at the proper time, that they are defenders of freedom, will, as we have said, be recompensed for the loss of their slaves with more than equivalent restitution, even though the purchase [of slaves] was not legitimate since neither was the sale of them, but we will excuse the complaints and offences that seem [to be relevant] even if they are not.

The fifteenth point: The naturales who would then not join in compensating for their ill-treatment throughout the kingdoms will remain subject to tributes and work levies, and in the same way the slaves who would not take part with their persons, administering supplies and food to our army (for which they would have to be paid) will remain slaves and so will the sons born to them. And masters who impede them [from joining the insurrection], aside from losing [the slaves] themselves, will be punished in their proper time and themselves become slaves. And, similarly, the sons of the Indian women who will not take part will also be subjected to the payment of tribute, even if their husbands do fulfill their obligations. It is just that they perform some work, since they share the benefits of liberty, the grandeur and comforts of all.

The sixteenth point: The naturales, free men, and freedmen, if they should merit (religious) habits, they will be given them with enough show of brilliance and the economic resources to support them, and the reports about them [of pureness of descent] will be accepted without any hesitation, for it is well known that they are not part of the Jewish race or any heretical (tendency), and the Spaniards who merit it will have the authorization through our grace, of having [the investigations] performed in our kingdoms, without having to go to Spain [for research in these matters], and we implore that Your Holiness permit us the same bulls, graces, and indulgences as are current in Castile and the right to award them and the confirmation of those [honors] that are accorded. And the same with the reports, and, for the Holy Office [of the Inquisition], information will be collected here as well as for other legal proceedings.

The seventeenth point: That the ecclesiastical benefits, bishoprics, canonicates, archbishoprics, and whatever is the responsibility of the king of Castile for nominations henceforward belongs to us. And for those presently functioning, let His Holiness then confirm them as well selected, and the vacancies from now on will be our responsibility.

And let the [administration of the] parishes be returned to the religious orders in the form and manner they [previously] held, and let them perpetually be theirs. And as for the alms they now receive in wine and olive oil, receiving it as fruit of the earth, let it cease and be transformed into landed property for the sustenance and expenses of their principal chapters.

The eighteenth point: That because I am in need of the holy prayers of the servants of God so that through them my intentions may reach their desired conclusion, I ask and implore, for their greater service, all communities, of male and female religious orders, to intercede with His Divine Majesty to illuminate [my way] and set me on the path to his greater honor and glory and the freedom and welfare of these vassals. And so that all this may proceed with greater impact, I vow and promise before our Lord God to give income and establish patrimony for the poorest and most needy convents as their patron throughout the kingdom and each year pay [the expenses of] a hundred poor and honorable maidens, either by me directly or through my intervention, and this as long as I live.

The nineteenth point: That the estates of the Marquis del Valle be confiscated as iniquitously possessed, and if there should be legitimate living heirs, and it can be established that they are [legitimately heirs] let them be given each year what is due to them, and while [the truth of their relationship] is being determined, let [support] be apportioned to those who are well deserving and noted as such among that faction.

The twentieth point: Let the archbishop chosen to be the inspector general be suspended from his commission and let whatever delinquents there are be freed and pardoned and the public jails be opened so that they can freely be released. And the same for those arrested by the Holy Office of the Inquisition, except for those who are rebellious and obstinate in their errors against our holy Catholic faith, and the sentenced relapsed be executed. The rest [should] be freed and registered in case they reoffend, so that the holy tribunal can proceed against them. And let the judges, palace court judges, and ministers of courts supplied by Castile throughout all of New Spain exercise their offices while they hold them and request new favors in accordance with their merits, learning, justice, and qualities.

The twenty-first point: That those who were in possession [of offices as] royal officials be members of our council of finances, the judges be part of the royal council, and let the palace court judges be judges for our new chancellery. The palace court judges that will be appointed will be promoted according to their merits, and then the remaining titled nobility and grandees of these kingdoms will be named according to their merits and their achievements in these matters.

And taking [all this] into consideration, attending to the infinite mercy of our Lord God and the intercession of his blessed mother, our Lady (may he invigorate and inspire this justified and heroic faction), we admonish and exhort everyone, of whatever condition they may be, that in all peace and tranquility they subscribe to the reason and justification proposed. And they will be rewarded with the utmost grandeur. And if they are opposed, it will be necessary (though with consummate distress in our hearts, so inclined to clemency, benignity, and liberality) to proceed with the military fury that is permissible on such occasions as this one and endeavor to reduce them by arms. Because there will be no way of avoiding manifest risk to our lives, which for us who follow [this course] will offer eternal reward for having joined with truth and pious exploits so as to shake off the tyrannous yoke that so many, so numerous afflicted peoples endure. And for those who would resist, they endanger not only the mortal health of their lives amid [the clash of] arms but also their eternal life, inasmuch as they are trying to interrupt [the flow of] fairness and truth, serenity and public peace and the common relief of all. Which heaven would not allow, for we have seen clear examples of good and fortunate success from the beginning of the world to this very day for those who inspire and undertake similar exploits directed toward the universal consolation of all, as they proceed primarily with the greater service of God [in mind], so that his creatures may serve him more faithfully, as freer, more content, more in command of their reasons, more restrained from vice, and more encouraged by virtue and justice, which is achieved through good government.

Blessed be His Divine Majesty who commands things to be as they are, in his honor and glory forever and ever.

[Possible signature, blurred by a smear of ink]

Document 3: Proclamation of the Just Judgments of God: May He Punish Whoever Would Tear It Down

In 1650, after eight years of imprisonment, William Lamport managed to escape from the Inquisition prison in Mexico City. He took with him copies, already secretly prepared, of a judicial complaint against the inquisitors and, during his brief freedom, affixed them to the doors of the Metropolitan Cathedral and at other heavily frequented locations and even carried a copy to the door of the viceroy's own residence. He was recaptured on the following day, just as he was planning to flee to Veracruz and go into the mountains to seek shelter with runaway slaves (*cimarrones*) in the famous town of Yanga. The Inquisition collected original copies of this complaint, which are now in the Archivo General de la Nación (AGN). Here is the transcription of one of them, handwritten by Lamport and affixed by the author himself to the doors of the cathedral.[1]

I, Don Guillén Lombardo, revoking (as I do revoke) the accusation that I made concerning my grievances before the just tribunal of God, do claim in his sovereign presence and that of angels and men that I did not accuse my aforementioned enemies, who are so iniquitous, in order that our Lord God could punish them in another life, but for their correction in the present one, because of the horrors committed under the cloak of secrecy and religion.

And so that it may come to the universal attention of all, I say that I, in the year 1643, accused the inquisitor Domingo de Argos

---

1. "Proclamation of the Just Judgments of God." AGN, vol. 1497, file 1, fol. 8r.

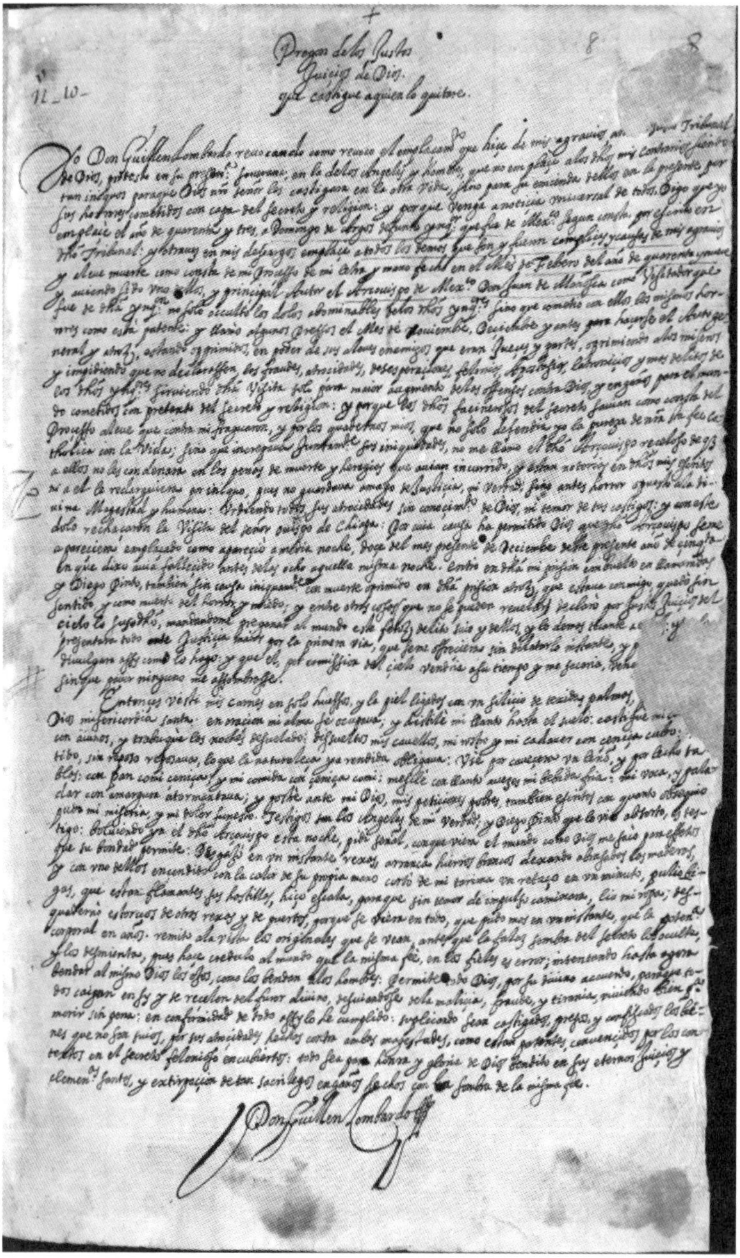
Pregon de los Justos
Juicios de Dios.
que castigue a quien lo quitare.

Don Guillen Lombardo

FIG. 4 "Proclamation of the Just Judgments of God." AGN, vol. 1497, file 1, fol. 8r.

of Mexico (now deceased), as is established in the written records of the tribunal. And, at another time in my presentation of evidence, I accused all the others who were both complicit in and the cause of my harsh treatment and [searched-for] perfidious death, as is stated in my trial proceedings of the month of February 1649, written in my own hand. And the archbishop of Mexico, Don Juan de Mañozca, having been one of them and the principal originator [of these accusations], when he was an inspector of the aforesaid Inquisition, not only hid the abominable deceits of the aforementioned inquisitors, but he along with them, as is evident, was guilty of the same horrors.

And in the months of November, December, and earlier he summoned some of the prisoners so as to carry out the atrocious auto-da-fé, [and they were] oppressed under the power of their perfidious enemies, who were both judges and complainants, oppressing the miserable and preventing them from declaring the frauds, atrocities, attempts to induce despair, felonies, apostasies, thefts, and other crimes [perpetuated] by said inquisitors. Said inspection served only for the greater increase of offenses against God and deceptions of the world, committed under the pretext of secrecy and religion.

And because the aforesaid criminals of the secret [tribunal] were aware, as is established in the perfidious presentation of evidence that they concocted against me and through my notebooks, that not only was I defending the purity of our holy Catholic faith with my life but also I inveighed against its iniquities, the aforementioned archbishop did not call on me, fearing lest that they should be condemned and die and [due to] heresies that they had incurred and were very clearly identified in my aforementioned writing, nor would they impugn him as iniquitous, because there was not [even] a hint of justice or truth about him, but horror instead and aversion to divine and human majesty, contriving all his atrocities with neither knowledge of God nor fear of his punishments.

And with this deceit, they rejected the visit of the lord bishop of Chiapas, for which reason God permitted the archbishop of Mexico to appear as present before me at midnight, on the twelfth of this month of December in the year of 1650, when he told me he had died before eight o'clock on that same night. Enwrapped in flames, he entered my prison. And Diego Pinto, iniquitously and baselessly oppressed with [the threat of] death in that same atrocious prison, collapsed unconscious as if dead of fright and fear. And [the archbishop], among other things (which cannot be divulged), declared by the just judgments of heaven the aforementioned, said I must proclaim to the world this vicious crime of his and of theirs and of all the others involved in this matter, and that I should without a moment's delay present this before a higher justice via the first means offered to me, and that I should divulge it through proclamations, just as I am doing. And he, on heaven's bidding, would come to me in [due] time and take me out [of prison], overcoming obstacles and any fear that might leave me astounded.

And then I dressed my flesh in only bones and skin, held together with a penitential shirt of woven palms, asking God for his holy mercy. My soul was busy in prayer, and my distilled lament dropped to the ground [as tears]. I punished my body with fasting and struggled through sleepless nights. My hair disheveled, I covered my face and corpse with ashes. I lay down, fully dressed for as long as [my] by now exhausted nature obliged, but without [obtaining] any rest. I used a block of wood for my pillow and boards for my bed. I ate ashes with my bread, and I ate my meal with ashes. Sometimes I mixed my cold drink with wailing, tormented my mouth and palate with bitterness, and I cast my poor petitions before my God, also written with as much courtesy as my misery and awful pains would allow. Witnesses to the truth of this are the angels and Diego Pinto as [another] witness, who saw it and was engrossed [by my actions]. When the same archbishop returned, that night I called for a sign through which the world could see that God had rescued me from prison [to do things] that his goodness permits. Instantly, he tore grilles apart, ripped up rude bars, leaving the remains of wooden clasps still attached. And, with one of these set on fire by the warmth of his own hand, he cut away a fragment from my cot in an instant; polished the burning, smoldering beams; made a ladder so that I could move forward without fear of falling; bundled up my clothes; shattered the hindrances of other bars and doors, so that one could see in everything [he did] that he was capable of more in an instant than physical power was in years.

I hereby implore that they be punished, arrested, and that the goods that are not theirs be confiscated because of atrocities committed against both majesties, proven by the confusions of information covered up in the felonious secret [process].

Let all this be to the honor and glory of blessed God in his eternal judgments and holy clemencies and the extirpation of so many sacrilegious deceits carried out under the shadow of this same faith.

Don Guillén Lombardo

Document 4: *Great Alcides*

Between December 1650 and February 1651, William Lamport composed the *Cristiano desagravio* (*Christian Ammends*), a seventy-three-page-long work in Spanish. He submitted it to the tribunal of the Inquisition at the beginning of his second trial, as an appeal for better conditions after his escape and recapture in December 1650. It is a devastating and subtle satire of his future executioners, which Rodrigo Ruíz de Zepeda (who would write the Inquisition's official narrative on Lamport's trial and condemnation to the pyre) described as a document of thirty-eight pages, titled *Cristiano desagravio y retractaciones*, "which should properly be termed reaffirmations." We are publishing a version of the long, untitled allegorical poem that prefaces the prose section, with the title of its initial words.[1] (Our comments on *Great Alcides*, organized stanza by stanza, follow the poem.) It is a grudging attempt to appeal to the inquisitors and includes an indirect admission of the sin of pride but without the least sign of servility. And Lamport compares himself to the great rebels and independent adventurers of mythological history: Prometheus, Hercules, Jason, Theseus, Phaeton, and Icarus. He addresses the inquisitors with apparent respect but from a clearly superior viewpoint, extending even to the epigram with which he begins the poem.

Among the most evident sources of *Great Alcides* are Ovid's *Metamorphoses* and the *Fábula de Polifemo y Galatea* (*Fable of Polyphemus and Galatea*) by Luis de Góngora. His knowledge of the

---

1. *Great Alcides*, AGN, vol. 1497, file 1, fol. 277r–v.

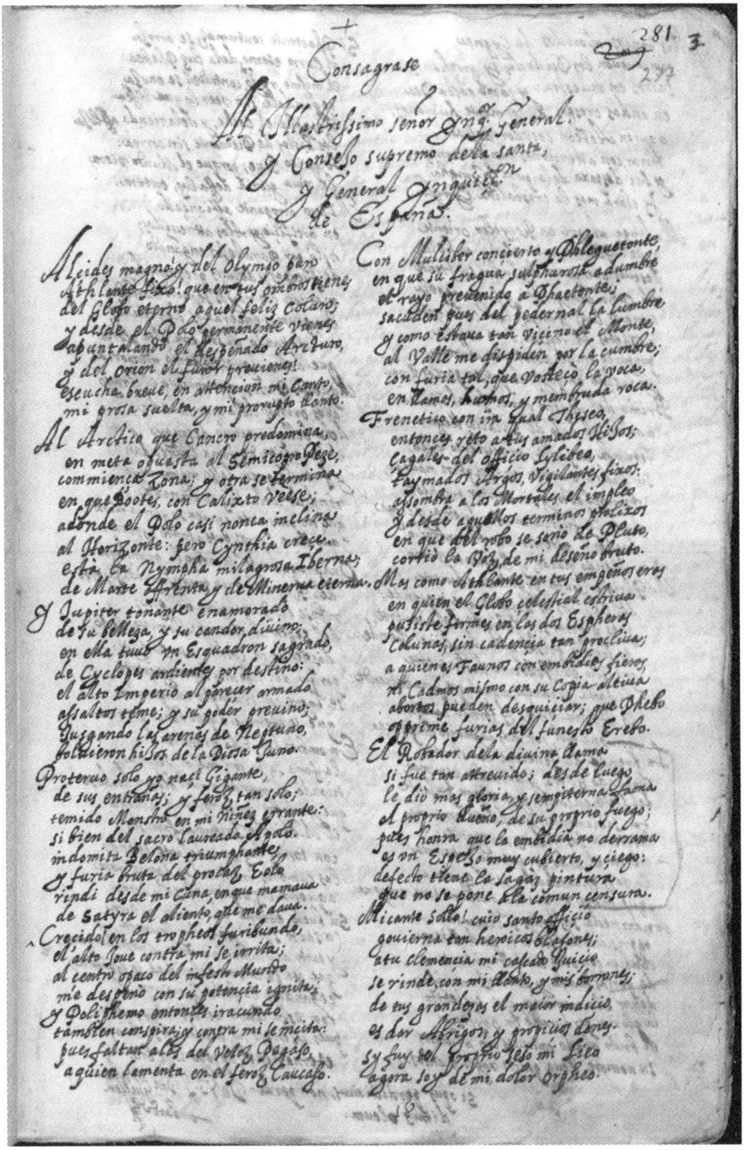

FIG. 5 First page of *Great Alcides*. AGN, vol. 1497, file 1, fol. 277r.

astrology of his time, Greco-Latin mythology, and classical literature is substantial, but it is not surprising that he makes some errors, since the work was composed in prison with no access to any books. In his epilogue to the *Cristiano desagravio*, Lamport declares, "I ask that those who understand and are knowledgeable to excuse the defects of my writings since everything is by memory without having seen a single book since I was sixteen years of age, when I exchanged [study of] the sciences for warfare and [concern with] the political situation."

Dedicated
To the most illustrious senior inquisitor general
And the Supreme Council
Of the holy and general
Inquisition of Spain

If the work was a waste [of time], the oil [of labor spent writing it] was not.

1
Great Alcides and Mount Atlas
fixed in place on pure Olympus,
bearing on your shoulders
the fortunate meridian of the eternal globe,
from the permanent pole you come
to prop up Arcturus who has been hurled down,
and the fury of Orion you forestall!
Listen a while, attend to my song,
my unbridled prose and the outburst of my lament.

2
At the Arctic, dominated by Cancer,
and at the opposite side from the Tropic of Capricorn,
where Boötes can be seen with Calixto, one zone begins
and another ends
and the pole almost never inclines
toward the horizon, but Cynthia grows,
it is there that the miraculous nymph Iberna lives,
dishonor of Mars and eternal Minerva.

3
And thundering Jupiter, enamored of her
beauty and her divine candor,
with her sired a sacred squadron
of Cyclopes ardent by their nature;
the lofty empire, though seemingly well armed, fears
assaults and forestalls their power
and evaluating the sands of Neptune
became the sons of the goddess Juno.

4
I alone was born from her belly,
a stubborn giant and nothing but fierce,
a feared monster in my roving youth,
although from my crib,
where from satire my breath suckled,
I conquered the undefeated and triumphal
Bellona, the crude fury of insolent Aeolus
and the sacred and laureate Apollo.

5
Raised on furious victories,
Jove on high then became vexed with me
and hurled me with his flaming strength
down to the murky center of the world and
then enraged Polyphemus
conspired as well and roused himself against me
because he who grieves in the wild Caucasus
lacks the wings of swiftly flying Pegasus.

6
In concert with Vulcan and Phlegethon
in whose sulfurous forge the lightning bolt
destined for Phaeton is foreshadowed,
they struck fire from its flint
and because the mountain was so near
they threw me from the heights to the valley
with such fury that the mouth of the forge yawned open
in flames, smoke, and hard splinters of stone.

7

Then frenzied with anger like Theseus,
I challenged your beloved sons,
youth of Lilybaeum,
cunning Argoses, steadfast caretakers.
My usage shocked mortal beings
and from those broadly ranging limits that
in thievishness were reminiscent of Pluto
spread word of my brutal intentions.

8

But in your strivings you were more akin to
Atlas on whom the heavenly globe is
supported. You established columns in the
two spheres free of any such rhythm.
For those fauns with their fierce jealousies
not even Cadmus himself and his freakish, arrogant
progeny can be upset, for Phoebus
holds down the furies of ill-fated Erebus.

9

He who was bold enough to steal the
divine flame of course proffered
more glory and more eternal fame to
the rightful owner of his own fire,
since honor that does not overflow into
envy is a mirror all covered and blind;
defective is the politic painting
that does not invite popular censure.

10

Glittering throne whose very heroic coats
of arms the Holy Office commands,
to your clemency my shattered judgment bows,
with my lamentation and my flaws.
The best indication of your grandeur
is giving shelter and kind gifts.
If I was, in my mind, my own Laius,
now, in my misery, I am Orpheus.

11

My harsh cries, like those of the swan Cygnaea,
move even the profane deities.
In appearance sacred, like the chaste goddess,
the sight of whom Actaeon, the hunter, sought in
the curling, sweetly human waves
through his desires, even if these were futile,
and the crystalline belt was the loot
from the pure nymph, though she was brighter still.

12

There dawns joyous in the rose-tinted east
that glory-desiring planet,
after fear sullied its brow
in its blackened birthplace,
and it calls then on a greater light
and grants greater brilliance
to Thetis, who distrusts the reflection;
purple vestments decorating the dawn
and turning into rays what she weeps in pearls.

13

That grim Nereus roaring in on the south wind,
whom the son of Salacia encounters,
resounds in his rage, truculent and malformed.
Her father then travels on a dolphin,
without attempting victory, astonished
to see power so powerless and blind.
Powerful, he disdains that opponent
who wears mother of pearl and variegated rubies.

14

The young, arrogant Phrygian warns
of his desired plunder from Colchis
because glory without danger of death is a
sad shadow offensive to glory;
since only the fleece gains this kind
of fame for him who understands fame
which is a living Hydra, for when its head has been lost
it begins to grow more, a thousand fold.

15
The beloved of faithful Penelope
plows through the gulfs and stirs foam,
because of the fierce enchantment, and his burgeoning strength,
so wisely and with such consummate craftiness,
arrogantly despising his hardships,
shuts his ears so that the enchanting voice
does not prevail, nor the siren
who kills through pleasure whom she does not afflict with pain.

16
Andromeda bemoans her sufferings
enchained upon the brown crag,
aided too by the waves, tries, with a
tomb of pearls and finest shellfish,
to leave behind an obelisk that will
sustain her everlasting glory.
The winged brute then with its gusts
carries her name through all the wandering winds.

17
If rebellious Phaeton went springing onto
the eternal chariot of Phoebus's light
that same lightning bolt was enraged against him,
blinding him so that he did not see what he desired,
and it hurled the chariot down, loosening
the diamond strips from the reins, without thongs.
Jove wished it, so that the world would see
the living glory of that total light.

18
Arrogant Icarus, who was supported
by artifice and daring wings,
flew through the parallels, in delusion
about his strengths and presumed intelligence.
But with the lightning bolts he found himself deceived,
the wax of his wings was melted,
and he fell, leaving such lofty glory
to the sun and his memory on the waters.

19
Of those goddesses, whom the Greek observed
on the seashores of the salted ocean,
the prince of laureled fame
was astonished by the beauty
and was the victim of the same lightning bolt
unleashed by that enamored light,
which does not consent that laurels be worn
by him who muses on glory, since he aspires too high.

20
The grandeur of the king of hell transformed
into a four-footed monster, a cold thing that
stole Proserpina's beauty for himself
and, attending to his kingdom and the scepter of
Avernus, settled the crown upon her head,
because from his theft more honor is achieved
more surely with so illustrious a triumph,
eternalizing that honor that is so rare.

21
On the shoulders of speeding Aeolus
let fame soar with greater resonance
through the world for the famous
Mexican tribunal, having already achieved
that fortunate honor through its divine virtue,
which with so much light rightly reaches
the intricate heights where dwells
that light, whom the sun adores.

22
Its eternal flight to the utmost height
(O sacred throne!) now raises up your light
and that pure torch is so radiant
that clarity itself is made afraid,
and even beautiful Polaris is blinded
by that celestial and sacred flame,
since Atropos eternally cannot deal
with its brilliance, nor can Clio quench it.

Editorial Commentary on *Great Alcides*

Each stanza in the Spanish consists of eight eleven-syllable lines and uses two rhymes in the following pattern: a b a b a b a a.

Epigram

Literally, *Si opus perdidimus, non perdidimus oleum* means "If we wasted the work, we did not waste the oil." William Lamport offers a variation, with a self-reflexive touch of irony, on a proverb cited by Plautus and Cicero: *Ne et operam et oleum perdas* (lest you waste both the work and the oil).

Lamport seems to be suggesting that his work, this poem and the prose that follows (*Cristiano desagravio*, which is introduced by the poem we have titled *Great Alcides*), is wasted on readers like the inquisitors, but at least the effort—the illumination he writes by, his pen, his thoughts, the few resources for writing that he has in his cell—was not a waste of his time.

Stanza 1

Alcides is another name for Hercules. This stanza and the two that follow present an astrological-mythological view of the birth of Hercules.

"The fury of Orion": The constellation of Orion, originally one of the Argonauts, is depicted in Hipparchus's and Ptolemy's second-century CE presentations of the cosmos as being armed with sword and shield as he confronts Taurus the Bull. Arcturus is the most prominent star in the constellation of Boötes (the Herdsman or Ploughman) located in the sky next to Orion the Hunter.

Stanza 2

"And at the opposite side from the Tropic of Capricorn," the translation of *en meta opuesta al semicopro Peze*: The astrological references to Cancer, Capricorn, and so on refer to the birth of Hercules, which is supposed to have taken place with the sun in Capricorn, the tenth sign of the zodiac, one week after the winter solstice.

The constellation Boötes (the Herdsman or Ploughman) was in life Arcas, the son of Zeus and the hunter Calisto (or Calixto), who was transformed by the goddess Artemis (also known as Cynthia or Diana) into the constellation of the Great Bear. Arcturus is the brightest star in this constellation. I have not found a specific explanation for the "nymph Iberna," though Hibernia was of course the Latin name for Ireland. The source of the "miraculous nymph Iberna, dishonor of Mars and eternal Minerva," may lie in a Latin myth that describes the unrequited love of Mars for the goddess of wisdom, Minerva. Mars asked for help from Anna Perenna, ancient goddess of time and the new year. But she, herself in love with Mars, took on the appearance of Minerva and, hidden under a veil, married Mars. This episode of female deceit was celebrated in the more ribald aspects of the Roman festival of the Ides of March. According to Ovid, whose versions of myth Lamport often follows, Anna Perenna was originally Anna, sister of Dido in the *Aeneid*, who drowned herself and was transformed into a river nymph named Anna Perenna.

Stanza 3

The Cyclopes lived in caves in Sicily and devoured human beings. Polyphemus, the strongest Cyclops, was blinded by Ulysses as part of his crew's escape from Polyphemus's cave.

This stanza has some obscure references. It is not clear to what myth Lamport might be referring when he describes Jupiter (Zeus) as "enamored" of Iberna or the reference to the nymph siring a "sacred squadron of Cyclopes." Unclear also is the reference to Neptune and the sons of Juno or the phrase "evaluating the sands of Neptune." We can point to only a few basic facts: the Cyclopes were sons of Neptune. The sons of June mentioned here are likely Mars and Vulcan. Juno was always inimical to the children her husband, Jupiter, had with other women and was therefore a great enemy of Hercules. "The lofty empire" that "fears assaults" seems to refer to the great war of the Titans against the gods, during the era of Chaos. The attempt by the Titans to take Mount Olympus by force was frustrated when Vulcan ordered the Cyclopes to forge the thunderbolt that would become Jupiter's personal weapon. It was employed against the Titans. Of course the feared assault against "the lofty empire, though seemingly well armed" would also appear to be an indirect reference to the Spanish Empire, with Jupiter allegorically representing the king of Spain.

Stanza 4

Bellona or Belona is the goddess of war and sister of Mars. Aeolus is the king of the winds.

Stanza 5

"He who grieves in the wild Caucasus" must refer to Prometheus (mentioned again in stanza 9), who was freed from his chains by Hercules. In this poem Hercules speaks in the first person in stanzas 4, 5, 6, 7, and 11. In the eighth stanza Lamport directly addresses Hercules, who is also the subject of stanzas 1 and 2. Only in stanza 10 does Lamport speak in the first person, directly addressing the Holy Office. Of course, the analogy between himself and Hercules underlies the entire treatment of this theme.

Stanza 6

Mulciber in the poem is another name for the divine blacksmith, Vulcan. Phlegethon is a burning river in the underworld. Phaeton, son of the sun, tried to drive his father's chariot. When he lost control of the horses driving it and was causing great destruction, Zeus had to strike him dead with a lightning bolt. He appears again in stanza 17.

Stanza 7

Lilybaeum is a peninsula in Sicily. The active volcano Etna is the mouth of Vulcan's forge. Lamport seems to use various elements of stanza 4 in Luis de Góngora's *Fábula de Polifemo y Galatea* (1613), which Lamport must have known:

> Donde espumoso el mar sicilïano
> el pie argenta de plata al Lilibeo
> (bóveda o de las fraguas de Vulcano,
> o tumba de los huesos de Tifeo),
> pálidas señas cenizoso un llano
> —cuando no del sacrílego deseo—
> Del duro oficio da. Allí una alta roca
> Mordaza es a una gruta, de su boca.

> Where the rich foam of the broad
> Sicilian sea plates with silver the
> foot of Lilybaeum (resounding vault

of Vulcan's forge maybe or, sealing
the rash Titan's bones, a tomb) there
is a plain whose cinders one may
see as a sign of either the sacrilegious
aim or of the workshop. There a
high crag thrusts across a cave's
mouth like a gag.[2]

Theseus is the Athenian hero, victor in numerous battles and a
friend of Hercules.

The Argoses were giants with a hundred eyes.

Pluto (Hades in Greek) was the god of the underworld and in
some traditions also god of the wealth mined from the earth. Here
Lamport seems to refer to Pluto as a source of wealth.

The conclusion of the stanza would appear to stem from a story
that Hercules, furious because Vulcan, on Zeus's orders, had hurled
him down from Mount Lilybaeum amid fire and falling rocks,
decided to challenge all those who opposed him, with "brutal intentions" that "shocked mortal beings."

Stanza 8

Hercules convinced Atlas to bring him the apples of the Hesperides,
offering to support the heavens on his shoulders while Atlas was
away. The "arrogant progeny" of Cadmus, the mythic king who
founded Thebes, would be the race of armed warriors, the Spartoi,
who had surged from the teeth of a dragon sown by Cadmus like
seeds in the earth. The "fauns" could be those who tried (unsuccess-
fully) to control the drunken Hercules at the wedding of Dionysus.

Erebus is a name for the underworld.

Stanza 9

"He who was bold enough to steal the divine flame" would be the
daring and ingenious Prometheus, who, as a Titan, stole fire from
Zeus as a gift for humanity. Zeus ordered Vulcan (or Hephaestus in
Greek) to chain him to a peak of the Caucasus Mountains, where an
eagle pecked at his ever-renewed liver every day. Prometheus was
finally liberated by Hercules.

2. Góngora, *Selected Poems*.

Stanza 10

Here Lamport directly addresses the Holy Office of the Inquisition, asking for mercy. He seems to refer to Laius, the father of Oedipus, who tried to cheat fate through his attempt to eliminate his son and flee his city but, on the road, met his prophesized death at the very hands of his son. Lamport identifies with Laius, both of whose stratagems backfired. And now, like Orpheus, he sings of his suffering.

Stanza 11

The hunter Actaeon had dared to watch Diana bathing nude and, as punishment, was changed into a deer and torn apart by his own pack of dogs. Cygnaea is another name for Artemis (Diana), the goddess of the moon.

Stanza 12

Thetis was a nymph of the sea, the mother of Achilles by Zeus.

Stanza 13

Salacia, the daughter of Nereus, took refuge from Neptune's lustful pursuit in the Atlantic Ocean, where the Titan Atlas protected her. Neptune rode a dolphin in pursuit of her.

Lamport's memory of this myth is somewhat confused. A "son of Salacia" plays no part in the myth.

Stanza 14

The "young, arrogant Phrygian" must be Phryxus, who flew on a divine lamb to Colchis, where the lamb was sacrificed and his golden fleece was kept, guarded by a dragon, until the hero Jason captured it. Lamport seems to confuse Jason and Phryxus, and neither of them are known to have been Phrygians.

Stanza 15

"The beloved of faithful Penelope" is of course Ulysses. "The fierce enchantment" would seem to refer to the sorceress Circe.

Stanza 16

Andromeda was chained to an outcrop as an offspring of the sea serpent (or whale) Cetes. She was rescued by her future husband, Perseus, who had with him Medusa's head, with its power of transforming any who saw it to stone (hence, perhaps, the reference to an "obelisk"). The "winged brute" may be Pegasus, the flying horse, born from the decapitated head of Medusa.

Stanza 17

For Phaeton, see stanza 6. This stanza follows the description in book 8, story 2, of Ovid's *Metamorphoses*:

> Whom Bacchus saw, and straining in his arms
> Her rifled bloom, and violated charms,
> Resolves, for this, the dear engaging dame
> Shou'd shine for ever in the rolls of Fame;
> And bids her crown among the stars be plac'd,
> With an eternal constellation grac'd.
> The golden circlet mounts; and, as it flies,
> Its diamonds twinkle in the distant skies;
> There, in their pristine form, the gemmy rays
> Between Alcides, and the dragon blaze.[3]

Stanza 18

Icarus, wearing the wings made by his father, the great inventor Daedalus, flew too close to the sun (against his father's advice) and, when the wax on the wings melted, plunged into the then-named Icarian Sea, as indicated in the final line of the stanza.

Stanza 19

"The Greek" (El Grayo) must refer to Epicurus, the philosophical inspiration of Lucretius's *De rerum natura*. Graius is the poetic name in Latin for a Greek, especially of heroic or mythological importance, used in the odes of Horace and also by Góngora (as el Griego) in his *Fábula de Polyphemus and Galatea*:

> Su aliento humo, sus relinchos fuego
> Si bien su freno espumas, ilustraba
> Las columnas, Etón, que erigió el Griego
> do el carro de la luz sus ruedas lava.

---

3. Ovid, *Metamorphoses*.

With smoking breath, and uttering snorts of flame,
the horses of the sun have moved away
to those gates the Greek erected, where sea foam
will rein them in and was the car of day.[4]

Stanza 20

Avernus was the name of a lake near Naples, supposed to be the entrance to the underworld and hence was used to refer to the underworld itself.

Pluto (or Hades) kidnapped Proserpina (Persephone). (The four-footed monster would refer to the black horse drawing the chariot, with which Pluto suddenly emerged from the earth to seize Proserpina). Her mother, Ceres (or Demeter), goddess of agriculture, overcome by sadness, left the world in permanent winter. Spring returned only when Ceres persuaded the king of the underworld to allow Persephone, now his queen, to return above ground for half of each year.

Stanza 22

"The sacred throne" is the Holy Inquisition itself.

Atropos, one of the three Fates, cut the cord of life. Clio was the muse of history.

4. Góngora, *Selected Poems*.

Document 5: *Regium psalterium* (Title Page and Twenty Poems)

Between 1652 and 1655 William Lamport wrote 918 psalms and hymns in Latin, concealing them from the men guarding him. He had neither ink nor pen in his cell, no books, no paper. He wrote on bedsheets, using chicken feathers culled from trashcans as his pens, and made his own ink from ashes, wax, chocolate, and other salvaged substances. Eventually the guards discovered and confiscated the sheets, but the judges of the Inquisition had all the poems copied, and it is to them we owe the complete preservation of these writings. Gabriel Méndez Plancarte in his 1948 edition partially published, studied, and praised this collection of poetry, titled *Regium psalterium* (Royal psalter). In 2011 an honors thesis by the Latinist Olivia Isidro Vázquez would continue this investigation, too long left unfinished. Méndez Plancarte's and Isidro's work offers us an insight into the literary and spiritual profundity of Lamport's writings. His poetry is inseparable from his profession of faith; it is the work of a deeply religious man who makes spiritual vows. At the same time it is the work of someone who wanted to free New Spain from the Spanish Crown and to liberate African slaves and restore indigenous rights, land, and status. *Regium psalterium* contains poems that are strictly religious and others that, though in a Christian format—the psalm, which is a form of prayer—and though always calling for due homage to God, refer directly to the condition of the indigenous and those in servitude. For Lamport there was no difference between spirituality and what we would today call social consciousness; respect for human beings of all races and standing was part of his Christian faith.

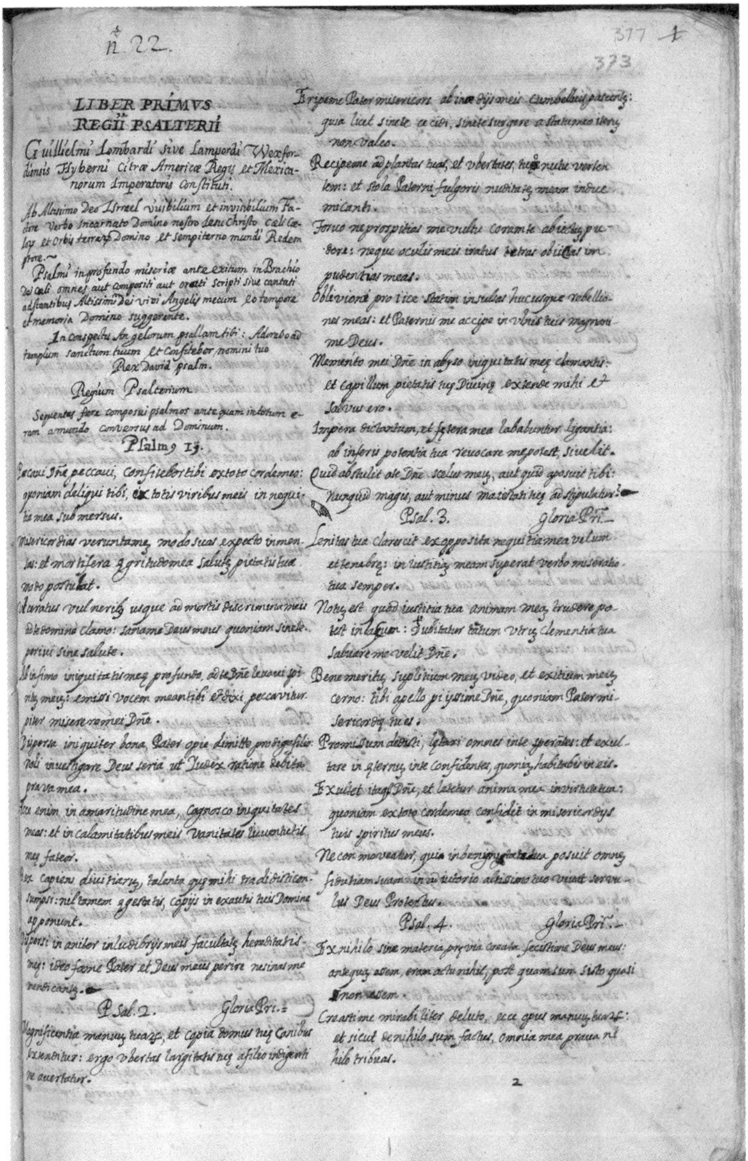

n. 22.

377

373

LIBER PRIMVS
REGII PSALTERII

Guillielmi Lombardi sive Lampordi Wexfordiensis Hyberni citra America Regis et Mexicanorum Imperatoris Constitui.

Regium Psalterium.

Psalmus 1y

Psal. 2. Gloria Pri.

Psal. 3. Gloria Pri.

Psal. 4. Gloria Pri.

2

FIG. 6 First page of *Regium psalterium*. AGN, vol. 1497, file 1, fol. 373r.

It is hard to convey the intensity emanating from these lines: his faith, most ardent and sincere, vying with his sense of desperation and a kind of mystical hallucination, in which he proclaims himself king of *America citerior* (Hithermost America) and feels propelled to a higher state of being before his "total conversion of the worldly to (the realm of) the Lord." This conversion is clearly registered in the pages of the *Regium psalterium*, where Lamport makes solemn religious vows and proclaims a kind of monastic order for the world, "the institution of evangelical justice."

Title Page of the *Regium psalterium*

Book 1 of the *Regium psalterium*

Of William Lamport, native of Wexford in Ireland, established as king of Hithermost America and emperor of the Mexicans by the most high God of Israel and of all that is visible and invisible, by Jesus Christ, who became the Word Incarnate, our heavenly Lord of the heavens and Lord of the orb of the earth, and eternal Redeemer of the world.[1]

All these psalms were composed or implored, written as well as sung, in the depths of suffering, before the finality of death in the arms of the God of heaven, in the presence of the angels of the most high, living God, the Lord inspiring me at that time and [for the purpose of] memory.

I will sing for you in the presence of the angels; I will adore your sacred temple and declare these psalms [to be composed] in your name, King David.

With justice I composed the following psalms before converting myself totally from the worldly to the (realm of the) Lord.

---

1. *Regium psalterium*, AGN, fol. 373r, title page. The translation is based on the original Latin transcription and Spanish translation by Olivia Isidro Vázquez.

Twenty Poems from *Regium psalterium*

I Have Sinned, O My Lord (Psalm 1)

I have sinned. O my Lord, I have sinned! And I will confess
 it to you with all my heart, because I committed crimes
 against you, utterly immersed in my depravity.[2]
But now I hope for your immense mercies. And my fatal illness
 asks for the cure of your benevolence.
Ulcerated with my wounds to the point of death, I call out to
 you, O my Lord! Cure me, my God, because, unless I have
 you, I have already perished!
Out of the depths of my iniquity, I have raised my spirit to you;
 I have raised my voice, and I have said, "In my stupidity, I
 have sinned!" O my Lord, take pity on me!
O merciful Father, pardon your prodigal son for the goods he
 has viciously wasted!
Because it is here and now, in my bitterness, that I recognize
 my iniquities, and in my calamity I confess to the vanities
 of my youth.
O King, who reclaims the riches that you gave to me! I have
 wasted the talents you entrusted to me, but my lack of
 these talents, O Lord, will not deplete your inexhaustible
 treasures!
In my vanity, with my games and jibes, I have squandered your
 inheritance. Do not let this beggar perish of hunger, O my
 Father and my God!
Glory to the Father, the Son, and the Holy Ghost! As it was in
 the beginning, and now, and always and forever and ever!
 Amen.[3]

---

2. The translation is based on the original Latin and Spanish translations of
Méndez Plancarte in his *Don Guillén de Lámport.*
3. This final line appears as a tagline conclusion to almost every poem and will
not be repeated at the end of the following translations.

Cypriot Mountains of Zion (Psalm 135)

Cypriot Mountains of Zion, gilded hills of Arabia, tall cedars
of Lebanon, splendid valleys of Elysium, and beautiful
orchards of Cyprus!
Air, fire, and water and trackless mountains of the earth! Scaly
fishes, flocks leaping through the fields, and birds of the
heavens bedecked with their feathers!
Amphitheaters of heaven and splendid mechanism of sapphire!
Stars glittering red with fear that recognize your Creator!
I urge you to speak, and I ask you. Where should I look for the
one I love? Where will I find him whom I love? Grant life
to your lover! Tell me, I pray you, where can I encounter
him who flees from me! And when all that I am is burned
away in so great a pyre, let what is me, within those very
flames, find eternal gentleness!
Ruby-red roses of Jericho! O palms of Cádiz that seem like
laurels! Rushing rivers of Babylon and always flowering
forests!

Why Do You Buy and Sell Men as If They Were Beasts? (Psalm 632)

Tell me, my faithful Americans, who claim to be on the side
of the Lord, why do you buy and sell men as if they were
beasts?
Why do you slay in slavery men who make their confessions in
the name of Christ? Why, against the law of God, do you
buy Ethiopians and not wish to be bought by them?
What power do you have over the freedom of your neighbor,
which is never to be sold for any gold? It is not permissible for you to hold possessions wrongly purchased and
produced.
They are born as free as we are, and just as they cannot be
allowed to make us captives, so neither can we be allowed
to reduce them to cruel servitude.
They are sold to you unjustly, and you unjustly buy them. You
commit a savage crime before the Lord. Freely make them
free men again!

Since their blood and captivity cry out against you to the Lord! If you do not, the scourge of heaven will descend on you and on your sons!

I Will Use the Name of King (Psalm 389)

Trusting in my omnipotent God, I will boldly sing out, and I will preach the glory of his power amid this misery of the world.

I will use the name of king. O peoples! Hear the mercies of the Most High! The Lord created a king from a miserable man and from a foreigner, a prince!

From darkness, death, and dung, God raised a humble man, and he shattered the power of the Demon and the snares of the world.

Still lingering in the sepulcher of death, I have sung these psalms, and I offer the future clemencies of God in heaven to the attention of the world.

The first king of the Mexicans was chosen by the Eternal Supreme [and] gratefully sings his praises to his King and God Jesus Christ!

Only King and God, my Redeemer crucified for me! I glory in your cross, and I despise the frail crowns of this world!

I follow you in your kingdom and consider mortal matters rightly abandoned! My love is for you, eternal treasure of life, in the realm of your glory.

Blessed Be Our God, the God of Jacob (Psalm 91)

Blessed be our God, the God of Jacob, praise for the living and true God! Who displays the power of his arm in heaven and across the earth.

He raised up the sky and the stars; he created the sun after there was darkness; he established the dwellings of the zodiacal constellations and sites for the fixed stars and the stars that wander.

To the sun he granted the power to engender imperfect beings like the worms, and he gave celestial bodies influence over what takes place under the moon.

The stars move men, stirring the mixed humors of the elements through which the supernal forces permeate nature.

The Highest, who created the stars, mostly gently moves those stars, and he who made us free men left us masters of the stars.

As probable, not infallible, the astrologers judge events, since nothing afflicts us for certain among the contingencies of the future.

God divided heaven into imaginary circles and gave fixed terms to the major hubs of the year at the apex of their division.

He displayed the miracles of nature in comets and celestial constellations and also in the extraordinary motions of inequality.

The celestial firmament and the power of reason signal the name of the Omnipotent to the pagans, and, for that reason, the evil with their idols are confounded.

Adore God, all you angels! Let us adore our God! And through his miracles, let us praise him who lives and rules across century after century.

May the Lord Rid Us of the Kings of Babylon (Psalm 680)

May the Lord rid us of the kings of Babylon and turn their statues to ashes, and may the Lord strike the sons of Nimrod with great confusion!

May he overthrow those who are stubborn at heart and all who despise the humiliated! May the Lord scatter the men of blood and those who spread iniquity!

May those who deceitfully testify against their neighbors and work evil with their hands be thrown into disorder! May those who trample underfoot the poor and weak be destroyed by the Lord!

My men of Spain, free yourselves forever from your arrogant pretensions. Do not despise my humble Indians or the poor Ethiopians!

They are as much the sons of God, as much the work of his hands as we are. The Lord is the protector of the small, and he will avenge their injuries.

Honor them and great will be your honor with the Lord and his
blessing! You will overflow with abundance in their land,
which the Lord has given to me for the benefit of everyone.

Jerusalem! Jerusalem! (Psalm 634)

Jerusalem! Jerusalem! Erected as a city that would be shared!
The Lord cries out, "I am who I have been, and I have sent
my Word out to you!
"He issued out of me, he who went to you! He who gave you
teachings and then again returned to me! I sent him to you
in the Word that left my mouth.
"I gave birth to him within myself, and I who have never been
born did not give birth to me! In him, who is another
me, I took pleasure, and from me, from myself, he gave
testimony.
"Erect the walls of my city desolated by your depravities. Be
sons of your fathers, who dwell in my vineyard.
"Why do you dress yourself in the plumes of my birds, and yet
you are the offspring of the dragon? Be my converts and
restore the ruins of my sacred residence!
"Perhaps you do not want to hear my voice, like that embit-
tered people of Israel! With your heart hardened before
my eyes, will you forever wander away from my paths?"

From Nothingness (Psalm 4)

From nothingness, no substance created before me, you made
me, my God! Before I came to be, I was not anything that
could act, and after I came to be I exist as if I never existed.
Miraculously you created me out of mud. Here I am, the work
of your hands! And since I was made from nothing, may
you attribute all my sins to that nothingness!
As does the potter from wet dust, O Lord, you fashioned me,
who am as brittle as glass. I fell and I am shattered. You, as
my Maker, create me again!
I was formed from the fetid, trampled earth, where the worms
live, and in the end I will be transformed again, into squalid
ashes.

Created in the corruption of rot, like a thick mass of spit, and
enwrapped by my own doing in another mass of spit, as
coarse as menstrual blood.
I was conceived as your enemy, polluted by the omen of sin,
and, being death that lives with life, I was born with life in
death.
If naked and in sin, my mother gave birth to me, how, unless
you cleanse me, can I put an end to the depravity laid bare
in my sins?
What am I when I entered the world, and when I leave the
world, other than criminality? Take pity on me then and
give for me on high. Give me your pardon, and I will live!

Creator of Heaven, Who Has Established the Axis of the Stars (Psalm 62)

Creator of heaven, who has established the axis of the stars!
You, who regulate the voice in strained throats!
O Guardian of your beloved and redeemed people,
freshen the songs of my exhausted voice!
And my tongue, trained by the example of your lyre,
will resound with your wondrous praises.
You shine in the sky with your golden gleaming,
You turn the dawn purple with your ruby glow
and with the beacon of Phoebus you remove the moist shadows
from the constellation of the goddess of justice, who has begun
to appear.
Through your gaze you bring life to all that is
germinating, and with your light you gladden all living things!
You gave the sun and the stars their changeable movements,
and you fixed as well the center of the pole.
You marked the limits of the days and of the nights,
measured out the months and the years.
By night, stars adorn the sky and beg
their lights from the wheel of the sun!
Like swimming fish, they course through the sky.
And to the heavens swinging loose without control,
you ordered them to be carried along by their own restless
lightness and to turn and return without end.
And in the same way you formed the earth with its weight

and set it motionless at the very center of things.
And just as what is heavy rests if it is not disturbed,
so what is light rises if not disturbed.
And you arrange the contrasting motions of the spheres of
    heaven
so that you alone may be known to be in power,
and, splitting them off from the waters that you created,
you formed those incorruptible spheres.
God! May you be eternally sanctified!
O Life, Glory, and my Creator![4]

With Only a Hair (Psalm 127)

With only a hair, O my God, you seize hold of our minds! The
    locks of your hair ripple in waves of gold that capture the
    hearts of onlookers with their living beauty.
Your snow-white neck is turned more brilliant by the touch of
    your ruby-red mane, and, with their rays of light, like a
    young fuzz of hair, they beautifully color your gleaming
    face.
You wear the diadem of glory, a crown more luminous than the
    sun, and your luminaries in the sky are overlaid with the
    most precious gems.
You are seated on the royal chair of the light, and you corus-
    cate—O Eternal Light!—on a throne of stars!
Your holy majesty is admixed with your beloved charity, and it
    stuns your blessed lovers.
You imprint strength, light, fire, love on our hearts and, losing
    consciousness, singing in eternal trance, they are swept
    away into you!

Shall I Not Openly Tell the World (Psalm 166)

Shall I not openly tell the world, my God! That I love you with
    all my soul! Or shall I bring to light the signs of love in
    my heart?

---

4. The original is written in rhyming Renaissance-Latin couplets.

Where shall I find glory other than in my God? Here I have
been, every day of the year, bathing myself in tears before
you, suffering for you amid my moans?

Sometimes I would mingle tears with my bread, and I would
score my cheeks with wounds. At times I would roar like a
lion in my lamentation! I would howl like a crocodile!

In darkness I wept for you, who are my light, and in a lightless
bed I grieved for you. I would sing, and the tears would
flow of their own will until they turned into rivers.

Mourning for my sins, I would carry you, O Life, in my spirit!
In your arms, I am flooded over with lamentation, and my
chest flames like Mount Aetna and launches groans as if
from a cave!

Thirsting for you, I would drink the flow of my tears, and, hun-
gering for you, I would give up my food! In my quest for
you, I am anguished by death, and my heart would tremble
with the paralyzing threat of violent death!

The Splendor of Your Hands (Psalm 2)

The splendor of your hands and the riches of your house are
available even to dogs! May the abundance of your generosity then not be withheld from your son in need!

Save me, O merciful Father, from my hungers, I who am
grazing with the beasts. For, although I fell without you,
without you I cannot raise myself up again from this state!

Receive me into your schemes and convert me, with one single
sign from you, to the enjoyment of your riches and clothe
my nudity with the replacement mantle of your paternal
brilliance!

Do not look fiercely on me, who am covered with shame in
your presence, nor in your anger do you throw my dis-
graceful deeds in my face.

Hurl into oblivion, conclusively, my foolish rebellions and
receive me, O magnanimous God, in your fatherly arms.

Attend to me, O Lord, as I call out from the abyss of my
depravity; extend to me but a hair of your divine compassion, and I will be saved!

You! Order it! Only say it! And the bonds of my crimes will
loosen. Your power may call me back even from the underworld, if you so choose.

Has my crime taken anything from you, O my Lord, or added
anything? Has it perchance added to or else diminished
from Your Majesty?

You Die, Eternal Victor (Psalm 121)

Crying out aloud once more with your great voice, you die,
Eternal Victor, and, bowing your head to the world, you
show your supreme clemency.

Five rivers sprout from the abyss, and, dividing the Red Sea,
you, our living Leader, open up a safe road for your faithful
people.

In the rejoined waters, the stubborn pharaoh and his army
of darkness is drowned, and liquid that flows from your
pierced side shows that your anger has become honey
sweet.

O fortunate for mortals, this day of so tragic a death, O war
waged by so many destinies and brought to its end with so
many divine laurels by the highest Lord!

Behold the torches of the heavens as they hide their rays in
mourning and the shadow-wreathed earth shudders in fear.
The temple splits asunder as the temple is dissolved!

The rocks are thunderously split, and blasphemous mouths are
stunned! Gravestones howl, the dead are brought back to
life, and all weep for their creator.

Everything in nature commemorates and laments the funeral
of the Lord, but none of these signs will move the blood-
soaked priests to faith.

The executioners confess that they have slain God; they beat
their bronze breasts, and yet they do what they do, and the
blind are led by the blind to their perdition.

O faithful hearts, dispend your tender grief! Weep for the
labors the highest God has endured for your sake and with
your outcries sing and proclaim the mercies of the Lord!

Grant Me That Which I Implore (Psalm 167)

Do, O my Lord! What I ask of you! And grant me that which
I implore! If you are with me, I pray that you never part
from me, and, should you go away, that you go not far!
You are the treasury of my heart. I have rooted myself in you
because of love. You are the light of my eyes! Because they
always see you resplendent, they meditate on you; they
search you out!
You are a divine honeycomb for my mouth; my lips taste of
you and, thus sweetened, they praise you. You are the food
that my palate consumes, hungry for ambrosia.
Your spirit is my essence, which finds life and motion in you.
You are the finest road for my soul, which both directs its
footsteps on your way and walks along with you.
You are the pleasure and the love of my free will, which glories
in you! That rests united in you! That finds ecstasy and
consumes itself in you!
You are the wisdom in my understanding, and in you my
powers of discrimination are nourished. You are the entire
force of my memory, which, through thinking of you con-
tinually, may hold on to you.
And, finally, you are the glory of my mind, which, absorbed
into you, is happy! And may it, with endless proclamations, join the chorus celebrating your great works!

Sing, O Slaves to the Lord (Psalm 633)

Sing, O slaves, to the Lord! After the transformation of your
servitude. Serve the Lord your God, you and your children,
and glory in him.
Remember the mercies of the Lord until the end of the age.
With his strong arms he tore you away from the yoke and
the house of servitude.
Be grateful to the Highest, since you have seen his great works!
Today he freed you, the slaves, just as he once freed Israel.
After liberation do not adore false gods as they did in the des-
ert! With true faith, adore the Lord God of Israel, who was
crucified for us.

Celebrate this solemn and memorable day across the generations. Bless God, who displays his power on our behalf.
Our God takes mercy on us and lifts us out of captivity. In the
face of the gentiles, he who is omnipotent snatched us free
from our enemies!

Intoxicated, My Soul Speaks to You (Psalm 171)

Intoxicated, my soul speaks to you, O Lord! I will tell you what
I desire, for I am clothed in love. You, my God, whom I
desire, you who can do so, fulfill my wishes.
I cannot feel what I should say; I am burning but I do not see
the flames. I discern the effects, know that you are the
cause, and, although I deserve nothing, your clemency
gives me great gifts.
And so I will say that it is not me who speaks, but your virtue
and your love that speak in me. You, my Life, you keep me
alive, for you also live in the bosom of me.
I bear you like a seal over the secret depths of my heart. I
feel you searching with fire through my kidneys and the
marrows of my bones, and, in the same way, your sweetly
burning pyre seizes hold of my entrails.
Either my own knowledge deceives me, or imagination makes
me stumble, or you know that what I feel is true, and true
too is that which I entreat, for my wound does not prevent
it from being felt.
You write on my tongue like the pen of a scribe. In my mind I
read through you like a book. And whatever I say that is
said well, you dictate it to me. And let the honor go to you!
And may you have eternal praise and majesty!

The Favor You Gave Me (Psalm 267)

To the King, my Lord, I will sing the new canticles that are in
my heart. On my lute, in exultation, I will sing your eternal proclamations.
First there was the favor you gave me! If I may be allowed to
reveal the gift granted to a man as unworthy as me! The
sight of her, who bore the divine Word!

The Virgin Mother, of serene and immaculate majesty, wrapped in a shining robe, that most pure woman manifests before my eyes. And, below her short blue cloak, she wears a gaily decorated belt. And the Virgin with her magnificent face brushed me with her robe.

And I, falling to the earth and pouring out tears, showed my adoration for the exalted Queen who is full of power and grace.

Mother of mercy! Fortunate Mother of God! Blessed Virgin! Remember this sinner and pray for me to God!

From My Very Beginning I Was Infected (Psalm 5)

At once, from my very beginning I was infected by original sin passed down to me, and then, I myself infecting myself, I have become, every day, disease itself.

Lord, you grant me life, which I fought against with death as my companion! And in this duel I subjugated myself to myself with my mortal weapons!

My free will overcame me, feeble because of the ancient ailment, and, always leaning toward what was forbidden, I lost my health and my power to heal.

Caught on the hook of sin, my understanding was plunged into all-encompassing darkness, and the blind power of my free will, through my own fault, was forcing me toward the pit.

The struggle between the two powers is unending, their confrontation is tireless, and finally my light is drawn toward evil by the darkness that offers the appearance of good.

My soul on fire—O the worse for me!—struggles with burning fevers, and when the blaze of the fire has died down, a spark from what remains bursts into flame.

The diffuse heat of my sins reins in my heart! Within my soul my sick soul stirs up the horrors of death!

I Am Assaulted by the Deadly Lightning Bolt of My Wounds (Psalm 11)

I am assaulted by the deadly lightning bolt of my wounds. O my God on high, my soul struggles with the final disease and the threat of collapse.

The danger of death most sad looms over me, and my tongue
trembles. Saliva thickens and clings to my throat and my
jaws.

You see roaring lions ready to devour my soul in their gaping
maws; they terrify my spirit with their claws and the blows
of their paws.

I will portray my death and the end of me! My eye will be covered over with all-encompassing darkness, and in my final
agony my glowing light will be extinguished.

My nerves and arteries constrict; the bonds of my ligaments
are loosened. Anguished by the turbulent struggle with
death, my breast swells with fear!

And the vital expression from my open mouth turns harsh. My
lips can produce only a grating sound that fuses with the
chattering of my teeth!

The bubbling blood flows through the pressure in my heart.
My pallor turns black, and the image of a corpse swells into
place before me.

An animal stench that issues from my belly drives away even
my most intimate friends! All who are greedy struggle for
nothing but accursed riches!

Daughters of Mexico! (Psalm 401)

Daughters of Mexico! Emulate the daughters of Israel! Praise
the Lord God of Israel, your King and Redeemer!

In the holiness of your heart, sing before him and glory in
him! Sing to the Lord with your lyres and dance with great
joy!

Crown the courtyards with garlands and sow the streets with
flowers! Decorate your houses with finest silks and hang
them with golden tapestries!

Offer the Lord fragrant unguents as he proceeds on the road!
Powerfully exult! Cry out, "Long live the King of heaven,
Christ the Redeemer!"

He will enter into the ark, a sanctified triumphal testimony. He
is no mortal king destined for the worms.

With pleasure prepare the festive offerings for the immense
Lord; his entrance into the city of the King of Glory will
spread throughout the entire world!

With so many high-minded signs of joy, let them celebrate
and glorify the divine King, since he will free us from the
iniquitous yoke of slavery!

And people will say, "Great God in his magnificence has done
lofty things for you! Nor has he done such prodigies for
every nation!" Sing it out!

Document 6: Excerpt from the Report by
Rodrigo Ruíz de Zepeda Martínez

The ceremonial trial and execution of so-called heretics in Mexico,
like the "general" (of particular size and importance) autos-da-fé of
"Judaizers" in 1649 and the one in 1659 in which William Lamport
died, were accompanied by the publication of books commissioned
by the Holy Office of the Inquisition, in which established writers
provided both an overview and a more detailed account of events. The
scholar Rodrigo Ruíz de Zepeda Martínez composed a 159-page book
on the 1659 auto-da-fé, titled *Auto general de la fee*. (He had been
appointed by the Inquisition as Lamport's official "defender.")

In the auto-da-fé of 1659, six prisoners were executed (in judicial
terms, "surrendered to justice and the secular arm"). As explained in
the introduction to the book, this auto-da-fé was a somewhat hurried
procedure, in large part motivated by a desire to be rid of William
Lamport. He was described as a "culprit" who had "plotted to raise up
the kingdom in rebellion," "famous for weaving impostures," known
throughout the city and responsible for inciting the Holy Office's
prisoners.

And when the day came, he slept all afternoon and evening, leaving
his cellmate to wake him, which he did after prayers.[1] And at eight
o'clock, when they had already brought him his dinner, he tore up
the grille and removed the wood balusters that descended to the patio
and helped his cellmate out so that they passed between the two

1. Ruíz de Zepeda Martínez, *Auto general de la fee*.

doors, and the accused set fire to the bars from the inside; cut through the main door and threw out beams, clothing, a brazier, bars, and whatever else they had need of; and escaped through the window. He came out to a path, where he had to break down the fence, over which he exited to the garden. He set fire to the bars and cut through them, and it was not necessary to cut through the turret of the garden because, in grappling with it he broke off a board that was part of it, allowing them to get out, taking with them beams and the clothing in two bundles, and, looking around the corners of the garden for the lowest part of the wall, they saw a raised mount at street level. And he placed a beam against the top of the wall, which was all he needed. He climbed up the wall, and his cellmate handed him the bundles, which he dropped down into the street, before he let himself down by a rope, which he tied to a battlement, and after him came his companion. Thus was the manner of their escape, which the accused put down to a supernatural marvel; leaving hidden, before escaping, all the instruments that he had used to accomplish his plan.

And at three in the morning, they arrived by way of Relox Street at the entrance to this cathedral, where he left his companion in order to affix two of his papers that he had brought with him already written, one to the door of the cathedral, the other at the door of the provincial prison. And, once he had affixed them, he went off to deliver another document of eighteen sheets, covered with very compressed handwriting, that he had prepared and addressed to the lord viceroy. And he encountered a soldier of the guard, to whom he gave the document so that he might take it to His Excellency, telling the solder that it had come from Havana and that he had brought it from Veracruz, that he was just arriving from Veracruz, and so it was very important that it should reach the viceroy, and with that the soldier, thinking he would be rewarded for bringing good news, did all he could so that the message would be delivered before daybreak. And so it was delivered to the lord viceroy. And the accused went back for his companion, and both proceeded to the neighborhood of Santa María la Redonda, where he had expected to wait for the result of the petition, and on his way there he affixed three further documents, one page each, to the cross that is called the Talabarteros Cross, at the entrance to the streets of Tacuba and Los Donceles. They proceeded on their way, seeking the previously agreed house, and, because it was so early in the morning, the Indians were agitated and his companion kept on going, leaving him alone there; [the Indians] moved to seize the accused, thinking him a thief, which he denied. He asked them to show him the house he was looking for; perturbed, he told them the owner's address, which was nearby, and, thinking that it was someone else, the owner of the house opened the door, and the accused entered, and the owner, not recognizing who he was, tried to throw him out. He calmed the man and stayed in this house that day. He changed his stockings and asked for paper in order to write a letter to the inspector general of the kingdom, to whom he sent another copy of the libelous writings he had left at the palace.

And he closed and labeled it. And very soon his host realized that it was not a good idea to have this man in his house, and—by nightfall—he moved him to the house of a friend on Los Donceles Street. And on the next day, when arrest warrants had been circulated with the description of the fugitives, he informed on the culprit, who was arrested by the first sheriff of the Holy Office and other officers, and he was put into the secret cells, with an ample guard.

All the libelous writings were collected, along with the one the accused had on his person. And to be noted is the stratagem of which he made use in order to write them and the manner he had for obtaining paper, which was that, with the money he was saving from his allowance, he from time to time requested tobacco and paper to smoke, which he did not use [for that purpose], and in this way he would have sufficient sheets, and the ink came from a few pieces of cotton from the inkwell that he had been given to write his defenses for his first trial, and, when these were used up, because they were not enough, he collected on a plate the smoke of a candle and, together with some drops of dark honey (which he requested for his meals) and water, he diluted the soot and brought it to the condition of ink, with which he could then write, and afterward he employed the same technique to write 918 Latin psalms on bedsheets, which [the prison guards] later found. And his pens were chicken quills that he found in his prison, sharpened with a shard of glass to such good effect that he was able to write all these works very intelligibly.

A second accusation was made against him, considering the libels posted around by the accused: that these were a collection of gravely injurious, scandalous, and offensive propositions directed against the Holy Office and the lord inquisitors. They were seditious, heretical, scandalous, and they incited Jewish heresies, for which he declared himself the author and presented himself at the beginning of these texts with the title: *Guillén Lombardo, by the grace of God, pure, perfect, and faithful; pure apostolic Roman; firstborn of the church; and heir to its purity dating back more than 1,400 years.* And he signed his name at the end.

And the aforesaid passed [a document] into the hands of the lord viceroy, of eighteen pages, also signed with his name and, presenting himself, as was his custom, with extravagant and heroic titles in his introduction. With overt hostility and the most abusive style imaginable, he descended to the level of circulating affronts, insults, slanders, deceptions, folly, daring assertions, falsehoods, and contumely against the Holy Office; its creation, style, and procedures; the secrecy it observes; and against the lord inquisitors, secretaries, and ministers. [It went on] in such a manner that there cannot be found a word not worth noting, not only for its insulting content but for its offensiveness against the purity of our holy Catholic faith, revealing himself as the author and defender of Judaizing heresies, as a dogmatist and rabbi of such ideas, teaching them and stating ill-sounding dogmas in his defense, with the flavor of heresy and very close to many errors, giving them credit, and accrediting his hostility against the Holy Office. [He continued,] saying that his zeal for the church and for His Majesty was well known, more than the Inquisition could demonstrate; and also saying that toward the public not even Saint Paul spoke in more Catholic a manner than he. And he sewed in many other doctrines and propositions on different points, heretic in form and in other generally considered ways.

And showing himself greatly repentant at having written and circulated such libels, since he had received no sentence for his offense, he strongly requested that he be given paper to write a retraction, and he presented a written text with the title of *Cristiano desagravio y retraciones* [Christian atonement and retractions], which should properly be termed reaffirmations, and, together with it a formal objection against the lord inquisitors, in a bold and gravely offensive style and more actively daring, he proposed that there should be an agreement putting an end to his case, setting a time limit of forty days to his request, and if this were not honored he would reproduce his complaints, for so he described his libels.

And he continued thus audaciously, when, during an audience in the presence of all the lord inquisitors, he launched twenty-seven propositions that he dictated in Latin, first justifying himself and saying that he was arrested for defending the faith and, then in the following twenty-seven propositions, not only did he show a heretical spirit, but they contained many heresies in the manner of the heretics Luther, Pelagius, Wycliffe, Jan Hus, and other heresiarchs, and some were the epilogue to whatever heresies can be imagined, and he asserted others opposed to holy scripture, falsely citing excerpts from the councils and returning to his prison boasting about having expressed them.

And afterward he presented other pages in writing, which he introduced with the title "Beati omnes, qui timent Dominum" [Blessed be all who fear God]. And all this matter, with the pretext of appealing to God, was an insulting libel against the lord inquisitors, contrary to the procedure of the Holy Office, against its practice of secrecy, its mode of judgment, and other features established by the holy church, the apostolic seat and general instructions, containing on said paper such detestable accusations and insults so full of poison that they opened whatever space was possible for the more than vehement suspicions about the faith of their author, and he described his heretical spirit and deeply held hatred of the Holy Office, because he everywhere presented it as cruel, tyrannical, unjust in its procedure, fraudulent in its secrecy, inhuman in its treatment of culprits, outrageous in its manner of arresting and examining witnesses and that the Jews and heretics it punishes were innocent, and all this paper was a noteworthy libel against the Holy Office and the lord inquisitors. And, specifically from the first paragraph until the eighty-fourth, he wrote many heretical propositions with his usual characteristics and, from paragraph eighty-five to the end, he wrote a lengthy conclusion to the paper in which, addressing our Lord God, he entrusts all his cases to him and professes that he is a sinner, but along the way he introduced himself as a staunch defender of the pure faith and of divine justice, citing this as the principal cause of his arrest, insult, and persecution by the Holy Office, in which he revealed his hypocrisy and could not refrain from displaying the venom of his abhorrence of the Holy Office because he declared, speaking of the lord inquisitors, this proposition directly opposed to the establishment of the Holy Office as an enemy of the faith justifying itself with a [mere] shadow of it. And in all the rest he offered a loose and disconnected motley of citations from holy scripture, calling attention through them at times to his ignorance, at others to his suffering or his patience or the tyranny of the Inquisition, showing his depraved temerity in offering and interpreting them in whatever he wished, abounding in this libel or satire against the holy church, against the apostolic seat, against the delegated ecclesiastical power, against the sacred canons, against the tribunal of the Holy Office, against the prerogatives of the king, our lord. And against the persons of the lord inquisitors.

And desperate [at being deprived] of paper to write on because it would serve only to give him the means to infinitely prolong his case and feed the fire of his inextinguishable anger and heretical fury, he decided to write a psalter of 918 psalms in Latin verses on a bedsheet, which they discovered when searching his cell. And the title of this demonstrates how vividly he retained in his mind the conspiracy that he was plotting, which this holy tribunal providentially cut short, because it begins with *Liber primus: Regij psalterij Guilielmi Lombardi, sive Lampordi Citerioris Americae regis et mexicanorum imperatoris* [Book 1 (of the *Regium psalterium*) Guillén Lombardo or Lamport, king of the Hithermost Americas and emperor of the Mexicans]. And this psalter was a continual narration and celebration of supernatural revelations, appearances, and miracles meant to persuade us that God had assigned him to be the author of this book, commissioning him to be the writer, prophet, and preacher for the purpose of defending the Catholic faith and evangelical justice, to create and govern a people that would have to live in great purity and the exercise of virtues, and he linked [these assertions] with the destruction of the tribunal of the Holy Inquisition because of the injustices and very grave crimes that he lays at the foot of its ministers, including extravagant improvisations, suspicions, and sophistries. With these so-called revelations he sought to earn credit and was weaving the fabric of his story with contrived manipulation, and he claimed to support his asserted mission as prophet and preacher as well as his revelations alleging that many cases were miracles that were [really] falsehoods and lies, so long as he thought his lies would not be obvious. And beyond the invectives, satires, infamies, reproaches, and insults that this psalter contained, his doctrine was generally impious and sacrilegiously defamatory, injurious, and sarcastic against the Holy Office; seditious, heretical, bold, and scandalous; very effectively seductive to simple minds; and dangerous and suspicious in [matters of] the faith. And he returned to defending and supporting Jews, heretics, and other criminals liable to be imprisoned by the Holy Office, and the Avicenna schismatics—opponents of the Roman and Catholic Church—and he filled the aforementioned psalter with heretical propositions, formalized, erroneous, bold, and with all the qualities that sacred theology assigns to doctrines opposed to the purity of our holy Catholic faith, in opposition to the good and wholesome doctrines received by the church from its councils, through the saints and the doctors, concerning predestination, the Trinity, the angels, sins, laws, grace, faith, charity, fraternal correction, religion, justice, the incarnation, and other matters. And unable to divest himself of his so deeply ingrained mind of a rebel, he revealed himself even more, introducing an assertion that His Majesty, the king, our lord's possession of these kingdoms was unjust, asserting that it was tyranny and because, in order to establish his treason, he needed to weaken the rights of our lord, the highest pontifex, he mixed in clear impugnments against the temporal power of the holy apostolic seat, like saying *that there is no Christian king who wishes to acknowledge the pope in any temporal matter and that Christ did not give that temporal [power] but only spiritual power to Saint Peter*, expatiating for this purpose on the [divine assertion] that *tibi dabo claves regni coelorum* [I will give you the keys to the kingdom of heaven] and *that neither [formulation] allows temporal jurisdiction to the pope*, making use of the citation that the impious and sacrilegious heretic Luther employed, who was followed by others in this mode of invective and opposition to the holy seat, and he considered it unjust [for the pope] to issue bulls for the possession of these kingdoms, and he clearly claimed to conspire against the king, our lord, in order to strip him of these kingdoms for being a tyrant and leave its election in the hands of the conspirators, through these words: *He possesses no [right to] action at all toward the kingdom, since neither by vote of the subjugated nor by the selection of our Lord God [is he entitled] to do so: it follows that it is just that anyone who would claim the kingdom in defense of our Lord God's justice and the poor should do so, and if—after the tyrant has been reproved—the vassals should decide to choose he who freed them as their king, such an election would be just.* And in this way that impious culprit qualified as unjust an absolutely evident right of the apostolic seat to give this kingdom to the lord kings of Spain and stated that whoever should take some specific action to strip His Majesty of power and be elected king had the justified right to do so. And all this was the consequence of the doctrine of the accused against the power of the pope and the rightful possession of the king, our lord, in order to promote sedition, raise riots, conspire, and impel these kingdoms to rebel, introducing such pretexts [for the rebellion].

He sought a second time to escape, trying to take the keys from the sheriff, seizing hold of him and attempting to take his dagger in order to kill him. He reached the point of totally losing his fear and respect, offending the sheriff and his assistant. He showed other very serious acts of disrespect against the lord inquisitors.

Finally, with his case established and concluded, he was declared a sectarian heretic who partook of the heresies of Calvin, Pelagius, Jan Hus, Wycliffe, and Luther and of the Illuminati and other here-siarchs; a dogmatist; an inventor of new heresies; an instigator; and defender of heresies. And [he] was delivered to justice and the secular arm, with the confiscation of all his possessions. And, at the time that his sentence will be read to him, he will justifiably have his right arm and hand raised and bound by his wrists to a ring, placed there for that purpose, and his mouth gagged, in punishment for having written the defamatory libels and falsified the seals of His Majesty as well as other legal instruments.

BIBLIOGRAPHY

Alberro, Solange. *Inquisición y sociedad en México, 1571–1700* [Inquisition and society in Mexico, 1571–1700]. Mexico City: Fondo de Cultura Económica, 1988.

Alvarez de Toledo, Cayetana. *Politics and Reform in Spain and Viceregal Mexico: The Life and Thought of Juan de Palafox, 1600–1659*. Oxford Historical Monographs. Oxford: Clarendon Press, 2004.

Armas, Frederick A. de. *The Return of Astraea: An Astral-Imperial Myth in Calderón*. Lexington: University Press of Kentucky, 1986.

Bayardi Landeros, Citlalli. "Tres salmos inéditos de Don Guillén de Lámport" [Three unpublished psalms by William Lamport]. Translated by Raúl Falcó. *Literatura Méxicana* 9, no. 1 (1998): 205–16.

Blanco, José Joaquín. "Retratos con paisaje: Los misterios de don Guillén de Lampart." *Revista Nexos*, no. 324 (2004). http://www.nexos.com.mx /?p=11356.

Bocanegra, Matías de. *Jews and the Inquisition of Mexico: The Great Auto de Fe of 1649*. Edited and translated by Seymour B. Liebman. Lawrence, KS: Coronado Press, 1974.

Chuchiak, John F. *The Inquisition in New Spain, 1536–1820: A Documentary History*. Baltimore: Johns Hopkins University Press, 2012.

Coffey, Diarmid. *O'Neill and Ormond: A Chapter in Irish History*. Dublin: Maunsel, 1914.

Crewe, Ryan Dominic. "Brave New Spain: An Irishman's Independence Plot in Seventeenth-Century Mexico." *Past and Present* 207, no. 1 (2010): 53–87.

Darcy, Eamon. *The Irish Rebellion of 1641 and the Wars of the Three Kingdoms*. Studies in History. Dublin: Boydell and Brewer, 2015.

Elliott, John Huxtable. *The Count-Duke of Olivares: The Statesman in an Age of Decline*. New Haven: Yale University Press, 1986.

"English and Scottish Planters: 1641 Rebellion." BBC. Accessed March 18, 2021. http://www.bbc.co.uk/print/history/british/plantation/planters /es10.shtml.

García-Molina Riquelme, Antonio M. *Las hogueras de la Inquisición en México* [The bonfires of the inquisition in Mexico]. Mexico City: Universidad Nacional Autónoma de México, 2016.

Góngora, Luis de. *Selected Poems of Luis de Góngora*. Translated by John Dent-Young. Chicago: University of Chicago Press, 2007.

González de León, Fernando. "The Road to Rocroi: The Duke of Alba, the Count-Duke of Olivares, and the High Command of the Spanish Army of Flanders in the Eighty Years' War, 1567–1659." PhD diss., Johns Hopkins University, 1992.

González Obregón, Luis. *D. Guillén de Lámport: La inquisición y la independencia en el siglo XVII* [William Lamport: The inquisition and independence in the seventeenth century]. Paris: Librería de la Viuda de Ch. Bouret, 1908.

———. *Rebeliones indígenas y precursores de la Independencia Mexicana en los siglos XVI, XVII, XVIII* [Indigenous rebellions and precursors to Mexican independence in the sixteenth, seventeenth, and eighteenth centuries]. Mexico City: Ediciones Fuente Cultural, 1952.

Greenleaf, Richard E. *The Mexican Inquisition of the Sixteenth Century*. Albuquerque: University of New Mexico Press, 1969.

Guigo, Gregorio M. de. *Diario, 1648–1664* [Diary, 1648–1664]. Edited by Manuel Romero de Terreros. 2 vols. Mexico City: Porrúa, 1952.

Isidro Vázquez, Olivia. "Himnos novohispanos del siglo XVII: Regium psalterium Guillielmi Lombardi" [New Spanish hymns of the seventeenth century: *Regium psalterium Guillielmi Lombardi*]. PhD diss., Universidad Naciónal Autónoma de México, 2011.

Israel, Jonathan. *Diasporas Within a Diaspora: Jews, Crypto-Jews, and the World Maritime Empires (1540–1740)*. Leiden: Brill, 2002.

———. *Empires and Entrepôts: The Dutch, the Spanish Monarchy, and the Jews, 1585–1713*. Oxford: Oxford University Press, 1975.

———. *Race, Class, and Politics in Colonial Mexico, 1610–1670*. Oxford Historical Monographs. Oxford: Oxford University Press, 1975.

Kamen, Henry. *The Spanish Inquisition*. London: Weidenfeld and Nicolson, 1965.

Keogh, Dáire, and Albert McDonnell, eds. *The Irish College, Rome, and Its World*. Dublin: Four Courts Press, 2008.

Kügelgen, Helga von. "La línea prehispánica: Carlos de Sigüenza y Góngora y su Teatro de virtudes políticas que constituyen a un príncipe" [The pre-Hispanic line: Carlos de Sigüenza y Góngora and his Theater of Political Virtues That Constitute a Prince]. *Destiempos* 14 (March–April 2008): 110–28.

Lizardo, Gonzalo. *Memorias de un basilisco: La novela sobre el poeta y rebelde irlandés que puso en jaque a la inquisición de la Nueva España* [Memories of a basilisk: The novel about the poet and Irish rebel who challenged the inquisition in New Spain]. Mexico City: Ediciones Martínez Roca, Planeta de Libros, 2020.

Lombardo, Guillén. *Cristiano desagravio y retractaciones* [Christian atonement and retractions]. Edited by Gonzalo Lizardo. Zacatecas, Mexico: Universidad Autónoma de Zacatecas, 2017.

Lyons, Mary Ann, and Thomas O'Connor. *Strangers to Citizens: The Irish in Europe, 1600–1800*. Dublin: National Library of Ireland, 2008.

Martínez Baracs, Andrea. *Don Guillén de Lamport, hijo de sus hazañas* [Don Guillén de Lamport, son of his feats]. Colección Centzontle. Mexico City: Fondo de Cultura Económica, 2012.

Medina, José Toribio. *Historia del Tribunal del Santo Oficio de la Inquisición en México* [History of the Tribunal of the Inquisition's Holy Office in Mexico]. 1905. Reprint, Mexico City: Fuente Cultural, 1952.

Méndez Plancarte, Gabriel. *Don Guillén de Lámport y su "Regio Salterio"* [Don Guillén de Lámport and his "*Regium psalterium*"]. Translated by Gabriel Méndez Plancarte. Unpublished Latin manuscript. 1655. Mexico City: "Ábside," 1948.

Menéndez Pelayo, Marcelino. *Historia de los heterodoxos españoles* [History of the Spanish heretics]. Originally published 1880–82. Buenos Aires: Espasa Calpe Argentina, 1951.

Mesa Gallego, Eduardo de. *The Irish in the Spanish Armies in the Seventeenth Century*. Dublin: Boydell Press, 2014.

———. "Irlanda y la política de la Monarquía Hispánica, siglos XVI y XVII)." In *Los irlandeses y la Monarquía Hispánica (1529–1800)*, edited by Eduardo Pedruelo Martín and Julia Rodríguez de Diego, 41–49. Madrid: Ministerio de Educación, Cultura y Deporte, 2012.

Meza González, Javier. *Laberinto de la mentira: Guillén de Lamporte y la inquisición* [Labyrinth of lies: William Lamport and the inquisition]. Mexico City: Universidad Autónoma Metropolitana–Xochimilco, 1997.

Morelos y Pavón, José María. "Sentimientos de la nación" [Sentiments of the nation]. Presented at the Constituent Congress in Chilpancingo, September 14, 1813. Accessed March 26, 2021. http://congresogro.gob .mx/LX-LEGISLATURA/images/Documentos/sentimientos.pdf.

O'Connor, Thomas. *Irish Jansenists, 1600–70: Religion and Politics in Flanders, France, Ireland, and Rome*. Dublin: Four Courts Press, 2008.

Ó Muraíle, Nollaig. *Mícheál Ó Cléirigh: His Associates and St. Anthony's College*. Dublin: Four Courts Press, 2008.

———, ed. *Turas na dTaoiseach nUltach as Éirinn: From Ráth Maoláin to Rome; Tadhg Ó Cianáin's Contemporary Narrative of the Journey into Exile of the Ulster Chieftains and Their Followers, 1607–8 (the So-Called "Flight of the Earls")*. Rome: Pontifical Irish College, 2007.

O'Neill, Elizabeth. *Owen Roe O'Neill*. Dublin: Talbot Press; London: Duckworth, 1937.

Ovid. *Metamorphoses*. Translated by Sir Samuel Garth et al. Internet Classics Archive. Accessed March 8, 2021. http://classics.mit.edu/Ovid /metam.8.eighth.html.

Palafox y Mendoza, Juan de. *Historia real sagrada: Luz de príncipes y súbditos* [Sacred royal history: Light for princes and subjects]. Puebla: Robledo, 1643.

———. "Sitio y socorro de Fuenterrabía y sucesos del año 1638" [Siege and assistance in Hondarribia and events of the year 1638]. In Tratados varios [Various treaties]. Vol. 10 of *Obras del ilustrissimo* [Works of the very illustrious]. 1762. Reprint, Madrid: Imprenta de Ramirez.

Pérez Tostado, Igor. *Irish Influence at the Court of Spain in the Seventeenth Century*. Dublin: Four Courts Press, 2008.

Recio Morales, Óscar. *España y la pérdida del Ulster: Irlanda en la estrategia política de la Monarquía Hispánica (1692–1649)* [Spain and Ulster's loss: Ireland in the Spanish monarchy's political strategy, 1692–1649]. Colección Hermes. Madrid: Ediciones del Laberinto, 2003.

———. *Irlanda y la monarquía hispánica: Kinsale, 1601–2001; Guerra, política, exilio, y religión* [Ireland and the Spanish monarchy: Kinsale, 1601–2001; War, politics, exile, and religion]. Madrid: Universidad de Alcalá/Consejo Superior de Investigaciones Científicas, 2002.

Riva Palacio, Vicente. *Memorias de un impostor: Don Guillén de Lámport, rey de México*. [Memoirs of an impostor, Don Guillén de Lámport, king of Mexico. Edited by Antonio Castro Real. 2 vols. Mexico City: Editorial Porrúa, 1976.

Ronan, Gerard. *"The Irish Zorro": The Extraordinary Adventures of William Lamport (1615–1659)*. Dingle, Ireland: Brandon/Mount Eagle, 2004.

Rosenmüller, Christoph. *Corruption and Justice in Colonial Mexico, 1650–1755*. Cambridge Latin American Studies. Cambridge: Cambridge University Press, 2019.

Rubial García, Antonio. *Profetisas y solitarios: Espacios y mensajes de una religión dirigida por ermitaños y beatas laicos en las ciudades de Nueva España* [Prophetesses and cenobites: Spaces and messages in a religion supervised by hermits and lay sisters in the cities of New Mexico]. Mexico City: Universidad Naciónal Autónoma de México/Fondo de Cultura Económica, 2006.

Ruíz de Zepeda Martínez, Rodrigo. *Auto general de la fee, 19 de noviembre 1659*. Mexico City: Holy Office/Calderón, 1659.

Russell, Diarmuid, ed. *The Portable Irish Reader*. New York: Viking Press, 1946.

Schwartz, Stuart B. *All Can Be Saved: Religious Tolerance and Salvation in the Iberian Atlantic World*. New Haven: Yale University Press, 2008.

Soler, Jordi. "Los orígenes de El zorro" [The origins of Zorro]. El País, November 29, 2005. https://elpais.com/diario/2005/11/27/eps/1133076411_850215.html.

Stradling, Robert A. The *Spanish Monarchy and the Irish Mercenaries: The Wild Geese in Spain, 1618–1688*. Dublin: Irish Academic Press, 1994.

Studnicki-Gizbert, Daviken. *A Nation upon the Ocean Sea: Portugal's Atlantic Diaspora and the Crisis of the Spanish Empire, 1492–1640*. Oxford: Oxford University Press, 2007.

Taylor, John Francis. *Owen Roe O'Neill*. London: Dublin, 1896.

Thomas, Keith. *Religion and the Decline of Magic: Studies in Popular Beliefs in Sixteenth- and Seventeenth-Century England*. New York: Penguin, 1971.

Trevor-Roper, Hugh R. *The European Witch-Craze of the Sixteenth and Seventeenth Centuries*. 1967. Reprint, New York: Penguin, 1988.

———. *Renaissance Essays: The Outbreak of the Thirty Years' War*. 1961. Reprint, Chicago: University of Chicago Press, 1985.

Troncarelli, Fabio. *El mito del "Zorro" y la Inquisición en México: La aventura de Guillén Lombardo (1615–1659)*. Lleida, Spain: Editorial Milenio, 2000.

———. *La spada e la croce: Guillén Lombardo e l' inquisizione in Messico* [The sword and the cross: William Lamport and the inquisition in Mexico]. Rome: Salerno Editrice, 1999.

Troncarelli, Fabio, and Igor Pérez Tostado. "A Plot Without Capriccio: Irish Utopia and Political Activity in Madrid, 1639–40." In *Spanish-Irish Relations Through the Ages*, edited by Declan M. Downey and Julio Crespo MacLennan, 123–36. Dublin: Four Courts Press, 2007.

Vázquez Guillén, María Bertha. "Tras las huellas del Zorro de Wexford" [In the footsteps of the Zorro of Wexford]. Master's thesis, Universidad Naciónal Autónoma de México, 2010.

latin american originals

Series Editor | Matthew Restall

This series features primary source texts on colonial and nineteenth-century Latin America, translated into English, in slim, accessible, affordable editions that also make scholarly contributions. Most of these sources are published here in English for the first time and represent an alternative to the traditional texts on early Latin America. The initial focus of the series was on the conquest period in sixteenth-century Spanish America, but its scope now includes later centuries and aims to be hemispheric. LAO volumes feature archival documents and printed sources originally in Spanish, Portuguese, Italian, Latin, Nahuatl, Maya and other Native American languages. The contributing authors are historians, anthropologists, art historians, geographers, and scholars of literature.

Matthew Restall is Edwin Erle Sparks Professor of Latin American History and Anthropology, and Director of Latin American Studies, at the Pennsylvania State University. He edited *Ethnohistory* for a decade and now co-edits the *Hispanic American Historical Review*.

Board of Editorial Consultants

Kris Lane
Laura E. Matthew
Pablo García Loaeza
Rolena Adorno

Titles in Print